ALL ABOUT HOUSE GROUPS

All About House Groups

PETER COTTERELL

KINGSWAY PUBLICATIONS
EASTBOURNE

ISBN 0 86065 361 7

Unless otherwise indicated, biblical quotations are from
the New International Version, © New York International
Bible Society 1978.

TLB = The Living Bible
© Tyndale House Publishers 1971

Front cover photo: Art Directors Photolibrary—London

Diagrams in text: Nuprint Services Ltd

Printed in Great Britain for
KINGSWAY PUBLICATIONS LTD
Lottbridge Drove, Eastbourne, E. Sussex BN23 6NT by
Richard Clay (The Chaucer Press) Ltd, Bungay, Suffolk
Typeset by Nuprint Services Ltd, Harpenden, Herts.

Contents

CHAPTER 1

Start Here

This book is all about running house groups. The house group is important because that's where the most effective teaching can take place, where the best friendships can develop, and where the best pastoral care can be given. House groups really *are* important.

One of the reasons for their immense value is the number of people that you get in the typical house group. It's because the question of group *size* is so important that this first chapter explains a bit about groups. It should help you to understand the rest of the chapters without a lot of boring repetition.

The four group sizes

Stand someone in front of a group of people and tell him to talk to them and you'll find that *how* he talks to them will very largely depend on how many there are present. If there are just three or four he will chat to them and very likely they will soon be talking back, asking questions. If there are five thousand of them he will probably want some kind of platform so that he can be seen, and some kind of amplification system so that he can be heard. And he may well talk for half an hour or more without anybody attempting to interrupt him.

7

Now imagine a speaker *reversing* those two approaches. Suppose there are three or four people, but he goes up on a platform and addresses them through a loudspeaker system and talks for an hour without a pause. Or suppose there are five thousand people and he stands somewhere out in front and tries to chat with them. Either way would be ludicrous.

The fact is that the size of the group *does* make a difference to the way in which we speak. Finding out how to speak most effectively, and studying how groups work, is usually called *group dynamics*. (I think I should add right here that group dynamics is not an underhanded way of manipulating people like a menacing Big Brother. It's simply a question of finding out the most effective way of talking to *this* particular group of people.)

It's usually recognized that there are four basic group sizes. For simplicity I have labelled them G1, G2, G3, and G4. Or we can call them *family-size* groups, *small* groups, *large* groups and *crowds*. The house group is a G2 small group, and has something between eight and sixteen people in it. The boundaries are quite flexible. The diagram gives a general idea of the four group sizes.

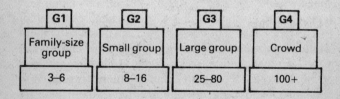

G1	**G2**	**G3**	**G4**
Family-size group	Small group	Large group	Crowd
3–6	8–16	25–80	100+

In fact, groups are a bit like woollies in the wash: they stretch and they shrink, they get larger and they get smaller. If the house group is a good one it will stretch, and may become a G3. That's a bit of a nuisance, though, firstly because the house gets cramped and uncomfortable, but more importantly because the dynamics of the group change. If the house group does grow then it is much better to split into two G2 groups than to turn into a G3 group. We'll see why a bit later.

Actually, the number of people that *belong* to the house group is much less important than the number of people who actually *attend* it. So if you have twenty people in the group but usually only a dozen or so turn up you'll still have a workable G2 house group.

At the other end of the numbers scale there's a different problem. If the G2 group gets too small it begins to take on the character of a family-type G1 group. What's bad about that is the fact that family groups don't like outsiders coming in. G1 groups are not growth groups. They tend to be cosy, enjoyable cliques which is not necessarily what was in mind when the group began.

So the genuine G2 house group stands between the G1 family-type group and the G3 large group, and it has enormous potential, precisely because it takes on all the good characteristics of both G1 and G3 groups.

Take the G1 family group. In the family you don't have one person doing all the talking. *Everyone* talks, including the kids. And again, you don't use carefully prepared speeches and polished language. In fact, very often sentences aren't finished at all. As you get near to the end of the sentence, everyone knows how it will finish, so, without waiting for the end they just chip in with *their* sentences. If you don't believe me, listen in to your conversation at home and you'll see what I mean. In the G1 group everyone talks, and they all use uncomplicated language, *colloquial* language.

In the G3 large group of thirty, forty, or fifty people, things are very different. One person might speak for a long time without anyone interrupting. The speaker may even have a few notes. He has his talk organized. Perhaps he's presenting a carefully worked-out explanation of what the Bible means by being 'born again' (Jn 3:3). 'Being born again' is a difficult sort of idea, and it *is* helpful to have someone work the idea out carefully and to present his explanation without a lot of interruption.

Unfortunately, most speakers in the G3 situation go on talking for too long, and eventually most of us find that we really can't keep track of the involved explanation. G3 groups do rather encourage, or at the very least allow, a speaker to go on talking for too long.

But the G2 group in a sense puts the G1 and G3 groups together and produces something different. The group is small enough so that, like the G1 group, we feel we can interrupt the speaker, ask him questions, use colloquial language. (You may have noticed the informal, G2 style of language that I have adopted for this book.) But the group is big enough so that the speaker can get in a reasonable length talk. 'Reasonable' here means reasonable for a G2 group, ten minutes or quarter of an hour. I'm serious. That is reasonable for a G2 group. Less than that in the G1 family group. More than that in a G3 large group. But not more than ten to fifteen minutes in the house group.

Actually, it's generally recognized now that 'lecturing' is one of the least efficient ways of teaching. That's very difficult for middle-class people who've been to university and endured hours of lecturing to believe, but in fact they probably learned very little from their lectures. Most of their real learning took place somewhere else: talking things over with other students, reading in the library, occasional seminars. This is the crucial feature of learning. You don't learn merely by listening. You learn by talking back, listening and then mulling over what has been said, and raising an objection, or asking a question or suggesting another way of looking at things. You don't *have* to do any of those things with a lecture. Or a sermon. You can just let the words float in and out of your mind without paying any attention to them at all. In fact that's just how most people, and I mean *most* people, treat sermons. That's why, half an hour after church, they can remember almost nothing of the sermon!

When real learning is going on there's a round of applause for a telling point, a groan at a rotten joke, a scowl at an unacceptable idea, a good laugh to punctuate a good joke. You will see people making a quick note. You may even see someone walk out of the room. That's all talk-back, *dialogue*. And it's a guarantee that people are not merely *hearing* but they are also *learning*. You can appreciate that it's much easier to have dialogue in the G2 house group than in the G3 large group. Conversely it's much easier to turn off in the G3 large group than it is in the smaller G2 house group. In the large group it is likely that no one would even notice that you *had* switched off!

So, a word of warning. Don't let the church make a decision to have house groups, and then appoint a leader who treats the house group as though it were a G3 large group. And talks for half an hour.

Another thing about the church's house groups. They ought to be mini-churches. A house group is different from the men's meeting, which is just men, or the women's meeting, which is just women, or the YP which is just young people. The house group *ought* to include men, women, younger folk, and older folk. A house group should be the church in miniature.

But what's so important about having house groups that are mini-churches? After all, there are other ways of forming house groups: with people who have some special common interest, for example. Of course these other types of house group have immense value, but they don't deal with a particular problem that faces many churches today: the problem of being too big. We have allowed, even encouraged, big churches to grow up, with maybe hundreds of members. In fact in America and Korea there are churches with *thousands* of members. But membership in that kind of church need be no challenge to the claims of Christ at all. It would be quite possible to worship God without even having to think about your neighbour. Even in a church with a hundred or so members it is possible to attend services (or 'meetings' as they are sometimes perversely called because the last thing you have to do in them is to *meet* anyone), without talking to anyone else, without getting tangled up in their lives at all.

But when a small group of Christians decide to meet together regularly, then they become aware of one another. The others take on character, personality. Each member of the group has the chance to hear the nitty-gritty details of the lives of the rest. And the Holy Spirit then *impels* them to get involved, to laugh with those who laugh and to weep with those who are sad. It's here, in the small group, among people we have to know personally, that Christianity is seen to be what it was always meant to be.

Non-Christians find it difficult to cope in the small group situation. They can manage reasonably well in a small group which just consists of *their* kind of people. But in a mixed group with a mixed and random membership— that's a different thing. You may have noticed that in everyday life people usually only mix with their own sort. Rich people in their clubs, poorer people in their pubs, golfers over here, tennis players over there, black people over *there*, Tories somewhere and Liberals somewhere else. All in their own little watertight pots.

Christians let the pots spill over. We're expected to become one family in Christ:

> In this new life one's nationality or race or education or social position is unimportant; such things mean nothing. Whether a person has Christ is what matters (Col 3:11 TLB).

In one sense the house group tests out what that verse claims. If it is true that whether a person has Christ is what matters then the house group will work. If it isn't true then the house group will fail—or perhaps develop into a different type of group, an exclusive group, who get on very well together and make sure that no one joins the group who isn't *their* sort.

Oh yes, it happens. It happened to the church at Corinth. The church *was* a well-mixed group, with slaves and free people in it, rich people and poor people, but they found this new society rather difficult. Paul's first letter to the church at Corinth gives all the unsavoury details of their many disagreements about doctrine, leadership, spiritual gifts and even the Lord's Supper.

But notice Paul didn't tell them that what they wanted was four house churches instead of one, so that each person could go to a church with others who thought exactly the way *he* did about everything. No, they *had* to learn to live together, work together and worship together. I think nothing less than the credibility of the Christian gospel is at stake. If Christians can't cross over some of these human barriers then what hope is there for the world?

We best learn to live this kind of life together in Christ through the G2 small group meeting in the home. There it's simply not possible to march in and march out again without taking any notice of other people. There you *can* learn about other Christians: their ideas, beliefs, fears and hopes, their families and their problems. And hopefully, out of this rich fellowship there will grow a true Christian family feeling that pleases our Father and beautifully proves that our Good News works.

HOW GROUPS WORK

G1 familiar	G2 small group	G3 large group	G4 celebration
4–6 people	8–16 people	25–80 people	100+ people
Like the family and some children's groups	Like many house groups	Like the average church congregation	Like large churches and crusade meetings
Everyone an individual because it's no use pretending	Very friendly because we know each other well	We all know one another at least by name	Everyone an individual because no one notices you
Language is informal, elliptic (we don't need to finish our sentences)	Language is a little more precise but mostly we understand each other and we don't mind asking questions	Not too many of us take part; you almost have to make a speech	Language is formal and you have to have a loud voice. Some speakers get rhetorical and quote poetry
The successful leader is the Mum or Dad type	The successful leader is more like a favourite uncle	The successful leader is confident and comes out of the same drawer as most of the congregation	The successful leader has charisma and a definite gift for public speaking.
This is where I relax	This is where I ask my questions	This is where I am taught	This is where I am inspired

Reprinted from *Look Who's Talking* (Kingsway Publications, 1984).

CHAPTER 2

What House Groups Can Do

First of all let's be quite clear as to what house groups are. They're not congregations that choose to meet in a house rather than in a special building. They're not primarily made up of people who can't find a church fellowship that really satisfies their need for learning, discipling and growing, and so on their own initiative invite a few people to meet with them regularly, in their home, for prayer and study and whatever. They are primarily members of a local church who are parcelled out into small groups that meet regularly in people's homes. They meet for prayer, Bible study, and friendship, and for a whole host of other reasons as well.

Of course there's nothing new about Christians meeting in one another's homes. Back in New Testament times they had to meet in homes simply because there weren't any special buildings called 'churches' to meet in. Very quickly they had discovered they weren't welcome in the Jewish synagogues. So they met in their homes. And now we're back to meeting in homes again. Some people see house groups as the answer to every problem the church has ever experienced. Others see house groups as just another gimmick which will solve nothing and which will soon fade away. As is so often the case, the truth is somewhere between these two extremes.

One thing ought to be said very firmly before we go any further. The house group is not just a means for pooling ignorance. If you know nothing about the Bible, and I know nothing about the Bible, and she knows nothing about the Bible we won't suddenly learn all about the Bible by meeting in a house group and pooling our ignorance. The rules of arithmetic never change: zero plus zero plus zero still equals zero.

Actually, failure to accept this uncompromising fact is the reason for the failure of so many house groups. If there's no one in the house group who knows anything about the subject being discussed, no one can give the right answers and no one can recognize wrong answers. A house group can easily become a hot-bed of heresy, a place where wrong answers are handed out and wrong advice given. Hair-raising things are said about God, the inspiration of the Bible, the beliefs of Muslims, and the Christian idea of creation, but no one says, 'Hey, that's not right.' Because no one knows that that's not right. From this point of view house groups may well be seen by some genuinely concerned vicars and ministers as being a menace to the parent church.

There's a more practical problem with house groups too. It's very difficult for the one-off visitor to find them. A house is a house, and looks just like thousands of other houses. But a church building—well, that's easily spotted. More or less permanent. You're not likely to turn up one week, only to find the church gone. But with house groups that's not the case. If a house group grows then it may decide to move to a larger house. And if someone in the home is taken ill it may not be very convenient to have a meeting there. And so, once again, the group moves.

So for one reason or another people may find the house group elusive. And then unless the newcomer is unusually persistent or the church particularly well organized pastorally, the visitor may never get into a house group at all.

But in spite of some admitted disadvantages, house

groups *can* play a powerful role in the life of the church—especially of the big church, where people may well feel themselves lost, overlooked. In the house group they can really get to know people, make friends, ask their questions and *learn*.

That last point is tremendously important. Christianity has been so appallingly presented over the past fifty or so years that very few people really know what it is. We have to teach them all over again the very basics of Christianity. It's not just a matter of learning the basic contents of the Bible, or a basic outline of Christian teaching, but a new appreciation of what Christianity *is*, what its answers are to the problems of human suffering and what it has to say about the meaning of life. We have to work at showing people fresh answers to questions about ethics: marriage, divorce, euthanasia, the poverty trap, genetic engineering and so on. Yes, Christianity *does* have something to say about these things, but people can only learn the Christian answers to questions such as these if there is somewhere for them to go with their questions.

That somewhere is the house group. A few of us learn a little from the Sunday sermons. But we don't learn very much. You see, the sermon is an attempt to say something that is relevant to everyone in the church. So the preacher isn't likely to be dealing with *my* particular problem. He might be dealing with what he *thinks* is my problem, but because there's no chance of any dialogue (I can't stand up in the middle of the sermon and tell him that I don't know what he's on about), he doesn't know how I feel.

And, of course, even if he did know my problem he couldn't really deal with it in church. And with two hundred or so people to think about, there just wouldn't be time to deal with all their individual problems in the Sunday sermons. Anyway, we'd all be embarrassed if he did start talking about our particular problems in public. Inevitably the preacher won't often be speaking directly to me. This is not to discount the Holy Spirit's use of the preacher's words in such a way that I am directly and personally challenged or uplifted. But it remains true that he is addressing all of *us*, not just *me*.

There's a most unfortunate consequence that follows from this. I switch off. I don't listen. True enough I have to hear the noises he is making up there in the pulpit, but most of us have learned the art of continuing to listen to what's being said in a vague sort of way (so that I can *look* as though I'm paying attention), but actually usefully employing the time thinking about something else.

The result is a monologue. He talks, but I don't have any share in the conversation. That's disastrous, because as I've already suggested, learning only takes place when we both share in the conversation.

Of course I might share in the conversation *silently*, by listening to what he says and thinking about it, and maybe inside me responding: 'That's right!' Or perhaps, 'What a load of rubbish!' or 'I'm not sure if he's right about that. I'll look it up when I get home....' Some people carry on the dialogue in that way. Inside. Without actually speaking. But a much better way is actually to speak out, to ask your questions, raise your objections and have the issues worked out there and then. Real questions are important. This cannot normally be done in the sermon, but it is good when preachers ensure an opportunity is given at the appropriate time.

That's one reason why Jesus asked so many questions: to ensure that the people were really involved, sharing in the conversation and not just daydreaming. See for yourself:

Which is easier: to say, 'Your sins are forgiven,' or to say, 'Get up and walk'? (Lk 5:23).

I ask you, which is lawful on the Sabbath: to do good or to do evil, to save life or to destroy it? (Lk 6:9).

Two men owed money to a certain money-lender. One owed him five hundred denarii, and the other fifty. Neither of them had the money to pay him back, so he cancelled the debts of both. Now which of them will love him more? (Lk 7:41–42).

Who do the crowds say I am?... But what about you? Who do you say I am? (Lk 9:18, 20).

What is written in the Law?... How do you read it? (Lk 10:26).

Which of these three do you think was a neighbour to the man who fell into the hands of robbers? (Lk 10:36).

Being able to ask questions is enormously important if we are going to learn anything worth while. And the house group is the place where most people feel free to ask their questions, because they are among a small group of people they know; people who won't make fun of them and laugh at their questions. And it is our responsibility to ensure that the questions can be answered. This is one big reason for house groups.

But house groups are more than just *study* groups. They are, or at any rate they should become, marvellous *friendship* groups. The very fact that the group meets in a house keeps the numbers down and that's important because tests show that although we can remember the names of seventy or so people when we meet them reasonably frequently, that number is too many for us to get to know really personally. We may remember their names, but we won't know much about them as people. We don't know the names of their husbands and wives and children and uncles and aunts. They're just names to faces. It's in the small group, up to about fifteen, that we are really able to get to know folk.

Even then it takes time. Time for the usual barriers to break down and for people to be reassured that they can lower the barriers, behave naturally, talk freely, let their hair down. Usually house groups are formed among people who live in the same area. That means you're likely to meet the others quite often: in the street, in the shops, at the railway station, or waiting for the bus. It becomes quite natural to drop in for a cup of tea, or babysit for them. Maybe your children play with their children.

So, the house group becomes a friendship group and also a *care* group. By far the most effective pastoral work in a church is done through house groups. You would think twice about ringing up the vicar just because you've got a cold, but when you do have a cold you don't want to have to go out in the rain to fetch the kids from school. It should be easy to ask Anne from the house group to help out. In fact you probably did the same good turn for her just a few weeks back.

And there's another great value in house groups. You can take people with you to a house group meeting when you wouldn't really feel so ready to take them to the church. People *know* houses and homes. They themselves probably live in very similar homes. So at least they will not be put off merely by the *place* where these odd Christians meet. And along the same lines: if the house group meets in your home, the neighbours soon know what's going on especially if you do a bit of singing. And then, when they get around to asking you what it's all about, it's quite natural to invite them to come on round next time, to see for themselves.

So what can house groups do? What are they for? For real learning, for getting real questions answered. For friendship and genuine pastoral care—even in little things. And as a means of outreach.

CHAPTER 3

Starting House Groups

So, house groups can do at least three things: they can be work groups where people learn, they can be friendship groups where people get to know one another, and they can be care groups where real pastoral work is done. Before actually starting house groups it's not a bad thing to stop and decide which of these three areas comes first in our thinking.

A word of reassurance here. You're not making a decision that will tie the church and the house group down irrevocably for the next fifty years. The role of the house group will be constantly changing. Sometimes its emphasis will lie in Bible study, sometimes in its friendship and sometimes in its pastoral work. The changing emphasis in the house group will reflect the changing situation in the church. If you've had a bit of a row, a real solid disagreement, then the friendship side of the house group can be very important in mending any relationships that might have been damaged. If some new doctrine appears and is being pushed, perhaps unwisely, by people in the church, then the teaching side of the house group may be invaluable in dealing with it. But when house groups are started, some questions have to be answered: what do we expect the house groups to do? Why are we starting house groups?

As we've already seen, large churches really *need* house groups primarily because of their value as friendship and pastoral groups. The large church nearly always fails on these two points, no matter how complicated a system has been set up to provide what is called pastoral care. The vicar will call, in the case of serious illness, or one of the curates, elders, deacons or whatever. And then there's a secretary somewhere who collects up all the information about people who are ill, and types out reminder cards for the clergy, who fill in visit-report forms when the visit is done, and everything is neatly filed away in a green cabinet.

But these systems depend on someone giving an alarm signal. Someone requests a call from the vicar and then gets it. But real pastoral work needs to begin long before any cry for help is likely to go up. Real pastoral care is in an important sense prophetic pastoral care. The need is anticipated. The compassionate heart of a friend, tuned in sympathetically, discerns a problem maybe even before the victim is aware of it. That kind of compassionate awareness comes from a much closer relationship than there can possibly be between a vicar and a congregation of three hundred. Or even of eighty.

So we may well decide that, to begin with at least, one of the most important aspects of the house group will lie in building up relationships—often called 'fellowship'. Getting together. Finding out what at least *some* of the other people in the church are really like. Getting to know their families, learning about the work they're doing, how the kids are getting on at school. Listening to some of the heartaches, bearing some of the burdens.

However, people won't go on attending a house group just for fellowship. Of course they *might*, if the fellowship were a little more concrete than is usually the case with house groups. If the house group only met to play Scrabble or Monopoly or to enjoy computer games, they would become rather like Bingo clubs, with a regular clientele, all of whom like Bingo—or Scrabble. But then house groups aren't meant for that kind of activity. And since they're not meant for that kind of activity they are not much good as just friendship groups. People quickly tire of meetings that are primarily a matter of sitting around drinking cups of tea and making conversation.

So then, even if you decide that initially a big emphasis will be placed on developing the groups as friendship groups, in the long term you will need to develop something more.

The house group really should be used for learning. This is not merely a reflection of a modern obsession with education. It reflects a biblical priority. Paul wrote a letter to the Christians at Colosse. He commented that he and Timothy were preaching about Christ. He went on:

> We proclaim him, admonishing and teaching everyone with all wisdom, so that we may present everyone perfect in Christ (Col 1:28).

What Paul wanted was to see the Christians at Colosse growing up. Becoming strong. And that meant *teaching*. This business of teaching was almost an obsession with Paul. The last letter Paul ever wrote was his second letter to his young friend Timothy. When he wrote that letter he knew quite well that his life was near its end—that execution could not be far away. So he poured out to Timothy the things that were uppermost in his mind as he faced death. And teaching was his priority:

> '... of this gospel I was appointed a herald and an apostle and a teacher' (1:11);

> 'What you heard from me, keep as the pattern of sound teaching; (1:13);

> 'The things you have heard me say ... entrust to reliable men who will also be qualified to teach others' (2:2);

> '... the Lord's servant must not quarrel; instead, he must be kind to everyone, able to teach' (2:24);

'You... know all about my teaching' (3:10);

'All Scripture is God-breathed and is useful for teaching' (3:16).

And again the very last chapter of that letter contains a warning that we should give careful attention to:

Preach the Word; be prepared in season and out of season; correct, rebuke and encourage—with great patience and careful instruction. For the time will come when men will not put up with sound doctrine. Instead, to suit their own desires, they will gather around them a great number of teachers to say what their itching ears want to hear (2 Tim 4:2–3).

Now why was Paul so steamed up about teaching? Isn't Christianity just a matter of going to church and leaving the clergy to worry about things like theology? I say no! Too much of that has characterized the past and it's just one of the reasons why the church is in the confused state it's in now. Note that Paul wanted to teach *everyone*. Not just a select few—the clergy. Everyone. Because no one is free from the danger of falling into error. If that happens, but the error comes from the only person who has been taught any theology, no one will spot it. That's precisely what has been happening. It used to be that the clergy were shocked by the unbelief in the pews. Nowadays the people in the pews, often brought to faith in Christ through school and university Christian Unions, or Christian fellowships out in the factories, or through evangelistic rallies, are shocked at the unbelief in the pulpits.

Now I don't mind being a sheep under the Good Shepherd, or even in the care of an under-shepherd, but I've no intention of allowing a chap with a clerical collar and three years in a theological college to determine what this particular sheep is going to eat. I mean to learn enough so that I can spot whether the proposed diet will make me grow or turn me into a mini-lamb. Or possibly kill me off altogether!

What's more, Paul was only doing what Jesus told his followers to do. To make disciples and to *teach* them:

Therefore go and make disciples of all nations, baptising them in the name of the Father and of the Son and of the Holy Spirit, and *teaching them* to obey everything I have commanded you (Mt 28:19–20, italics mine).

So house groups can take a major responsibility for teaching. Of course it is important that the teaching should be relevant to the particular group. Some house groups may be able to cope with and even enjoy a boiled-down university course in theology. But most house groups don't need it and won't take it. So the churches that are using house groups for teaching will need to spend a good deal of time finding out what ought to be taught in *their* house groups, finding out the questions that the people are actually asking. And then carefully planning the teaching programme of the church so that through the Sunday services *and* the house groups, and any other teaching groups that the church sets going, those questions are honestly faced and correctly answered.

The primary task

There has to be a decision taken about the primary task of the house group. This doesn't mean the group isn't allowed to do anything else, but it does fix a priority.

Let's assume that a decision has been made that the primary task for the house groups at the moment should be teaching. That primary task next needs more careful definition. It is all too easy to write down the primary task of the house group as 'to study the Bible', and then assume that so long as a passage from the Bible is set for study each time the house group meets, perhaps also supplying a few notes for the group to use, that the primary task is being carried out. But 'to study the Bible' is unsatisfactory as the definition of the task. Is it true that it is enough for the group to 'study the Bible'? Is this necessarily a help to them?

Let me illustrate with a story that has rather delighted me. There used to be a preacher with a very impressive voice, a very large vocabulary and a very forceful character. Preaching in rather a large church he was in full flight. He wasn't, in fact, saying very much, but it all sounded very impressive. His subject was the truth. The *terruuth* as he pronounced it. He went on at great length about the nobility of the terruuth and the validity of the search for the terruuth. And so to his climax: 'And what could be greater than to search for the terruuth?'

The question was rhetorical. However, the bubble was well and truly burst by a little old lady sitting near the front who responded sharply and loudly: 'Why, to *find* it of course!'

So what could be greater than to study the Bible? Well, to *learn* something from it. It really is possible to study the Bible without learning anything at all. Anyone who has spent time before an examination seated in a library with a great big tome open in front of him, desperately reading page after page, will know the frustration of finding afterwards that none of it has stuck. Probably because what was being studied simply didn't relate to him and so he couldn't latch on to what the book was saying. The same really can be true of Bible study too. If the bit being studied doesn't relate to me and my life, the things I do and the questions I ask, then I may well find that I have studied the Bible without learning anything.

So let's look again at our definition of the primary task. What is needed is to take the general aim of 'studying the Bible' and then to focus it down so that it's a bit more precise. We might focus on 'to learn what the Bible teaches about prayer'. Or we could be even more precise and express the aim as 'to learn why some of our prayer requests are not granted'. Instead of 'to study the parable of the prodigal son' we might go for 'to find out the practical meaning of the parable of the prodigal son for today'. Instead of studying, say, 1 Corinthians 11:17–34 (which is about the Communion service in the church at Corinth), I might decide that a more practical aim would be 'to find out why we conduct communion the way we do in our church'. Or you might want something more general like 'to learn how to use a concordance'. No, I know that some people won't even have a concordance, much less want to learn how to use one, but some house groups might want to learn that particular skill. In fact, a house group that I had in Africa particularly asked me to teach them how to use a concordance. Again, you might want to tackle a subject like pacifism. 'To find out what the Bible has to say about war and about pacifism' would certainly take more than one week if the whole vast subject was to be presented adequately.

Now, if you do sharpen up the focus of the primary task in this way you should find it easier afterwards to find out whether or not the task was carried out and the goal reached. Did the group learn to use a concordance? Was there later evidence that they were finding this bit of knowledge useful? Did the group see why sometimes our prayer requests are misguided, selfish, and so can't be granted? On the positive side did they realize that prayer isn't a ten pence in the slot machine: prayer requests in at one end and a guaranteed response if you pull the right drawer open, or check the appropriate box.

Incidentally, on the subject of prayer, I was appalled to receive (unsolicited) through the post the other day a magazine devoted to the principle that health, success and prosperity were the undisputed right of every Christian. The magazine came complete with a check-list of what you might be wanting God to give you, including boxes for a new car, a better home and extra money. Then you send in the completed form and the Foundation will pray for you and it, daily. There's another box to indicate how much you're sending as your donation to the Foundation. And by the way, if you send in fifty dollars or more, you get a *free* (I like that) paperback and six cassettes.

Christians need to be protected from this kind of approach, by learning the right use of prayer.

Probably the worst primary task is 'to have a house group meeting'. That particular goal will be achieved even if only one person turns up at the designated spot. Yet sadly that is the only real goal, the only primary task, that really exists for many house groups. Just to have a meeting. It's no wonder that so many house groups are begun with high hopes and with good numbers, but gradually the high hopes disappear, the numbers dwindle and eventually, mercifully, the group dies.

How to group

So far I've rather assumed that house groups are simply formed by dividing the people who come to church into groups roughly according to where they live. Then everyone who lives in the high-rise flats goes to one house group, everyone who lives on the industrial estate goes to another and all those who live over to the north of the church go to another. That is the most common way of organizing house groups. They're called *area* house groups.

But that isn't the only way. You can also have *interest* groups, groups of people who share some common interest. They might all be teachers. Or parents. Or single people. Or Senior Citizens. They have something in common and so they are likely to have some common problems, problems that might not be of much interest to other people in the church. Possibly, for that very reason, their problems never get tackled by the church. The Church Education Programme (CEP) must find a place to deal with these special concerns. (We'll look at the importance of the Church Education Programme later on in more detail.)

A special type of interest group is the *age* group. It's useful to have house groups for people from the same age-range. The teens, for example, have special problems, and so do the twenties, and the thirties and the forties and so on right through life. A church might well want to set up some house groups catering for particular age groups. This step could be particularly important for those churches which are attracting large numbers of people at the lower end of adult life: eighteen up into the thirties. Very often these people *need* to be divided up a bit so that they can get to know some of the other folks of their age group who also are in the church.

Churches with a large number of young people should especially note this need. Many young people's groups in the large churches have very good recreational programmes, but very poor teaching programmes. Often the teaching programmes that do exist are scrabbled together without any discussion with the minister, and may even be given without anyone present who is really qualified to do the teaching. So you have desperately needy sheep with untrained shepherds. No wonder the casualty rate is so high that few churches have any method of checking up on the progress of young people brought to them. The results of such a check-up would be too depressing.

How many of these house groups are we going to have? Don't worry, we're not proposing that every kind of house group should meet every week. Here's another important principle: no house group need be a permanent fixture. It can take a break. It need only meet for a few weeks. It can pack up altogether. Why not? Christians do seem to suffer from the delusion that to stop doing anything that the church has once started is to admit defeat. Nonsense! Stop anything once you've been convinced that it has served its purpose.

You can start Tuesday night house groups for young people and stop them after three months, because in three months you will probably have said all that they need just now. If you do decide to carry on you may well find yourself inventing subjects for discussion. Don't be afraid to set up house groups for a particular group of people, or to study a particular subject, and then to shut them down. Firmly.

For example, take solvent abuse—glue sniffing. If that becomes a problem in your area you may well want a month of house group meetings for parents and perhaps a parallel set of meetings for the kids. And then close those house groups.

One final point. House groups can often do very well what some of the existing groups in the church do rather badly. If that's the case then it's necessary to close down the surplus meetings. We can't keep on adding new meetings indefinitely without closing something somewhere else. Already we have a real problem with too many Christians spending too much time at church and too little time trying to be salt in the world. Too little time to give to their own families; too little time to give to their neighbours. House groups tacked on to an already over-full church diary could prove the last straw for some Christians. Look at your church's programme—and don't be afraid to use the pruning knife!

CHECK SHEET NUMBER ONE
Before you go any further, try answering these questions. The answers will all be found in the first three chapters of this book.

1. How many people might we have in a G2 house group?

    from _____ to _____

2. For about how long should the 'speaker' in a G2 house group speak?

    5 minutes _____
    10 minutes _____
    20 minutes _____
    30 minutes _____

3. We don't learn just by listening. So how do we learn?

    by reading _____
    by talking back _____
    by making notes _____

4. Can you find an example of a house church in your Bible?

    Place _____
    Reference _____

5. House groups are a mixture of three types of group. What are they?

    a) _____
    b) _____
    c) _____

6. Write out the 'Great Commission' Jesus gave to his followers just after the resurrection (Mt 28:19–20)

    _____
    _____
    _____

7. Write down what you think the *primary task* was of the last house group you attended _____

    _____

    OR

    Write down what you think the primary task might be for a house group that was studying Matthew 22:15–22 ('Paying taxes to Caesar')

    _____

CHAPTER 4

Leadership

We turn next to a key decision: who is to lead the house group? Oddly enough, it's probably an even more important decision than deciding what the group is to study. A good leader can even overcome the disadvantage of a boring curriculum. He'll make it interesting and relevant. On the other hand a poor leader can take the most vital and interesting of topics and make it as exciting as cold porridge on a December morning.

For the sake of simplicity let's assume you have decided to meet at the same house each time the group meets. That's much more sensible than trying to move around from house to house 'to give everyone a turn'. Do that and some of us are sure to forget where it's supposed to be this week, and since we can't be bothered to find out we simply give it a miss this week—and next week.

Let's assume also that you've decided to meet regularly and on a memorable day. By that I don't mean annually on April Fool's day, but weekly on Thursday or perhaps monthly on the first Thursday of the month. But not something complicated like every other week alternating between Tuesdays and Thursdays, except when there are five Tuesdays in the month when we'll miss out the second Tuesday but meet on the fifth, although not during school holidays....

So we come to considering leadership. Let's start by disposing of the idea that *one* person necessarily is in charge. It's just possible one person will arrange everything, but it's much more likely that you'll need two or even three people. One person to be responsible for the hospitality side of things, another to lead the study side and someone else to attend to the prayer session, if you decide to include that.

The actual gifts needed for these three leadership tasks are quite different from one another, and that's why I would not expect one person to lead each aspect of the house group meeting.

Let's look at each of these leadership tasks individually.

The hospitality leader

The golden rule in considering the appointment of a hospitality leader is to avoid anyone who makes a fuss. You know, the kind of person who does everything superbly, but makes sure that everyone knows all about the difficulties and everyone feels a little bit guilty about causing so much of an 'upsetment'. They recite every detail, and give a meticulous account of what was involved in preparing everything, and each so-called catastrophe that occurred. The 'no-problem person' is the sort of person you are looking for.

I first learned about the no-problem person millions of years ago from a *Readers Digest* article, about a man trying to buy a hat. In the first shop, the assistant is bored, uninterested. Rather unwillingly he brings out a few bowler hats. The customer says: 'But I don't want a bowler hat. I want something less formal.' The assistant is unimpressed: 'Well, sir, we do have some others, but they don't appear to be on display just now.' With much prodding, accompanied by much grunting they are at last produced. They are all the same colour: light grey. The customer asks if there are no other colours. It appears there *might* be, but the assistant shows no inclination to produce them. 'Look,' says the customer, 'these are a possibility, but the hat band is the wrong colour. Do you think you could....' A freezing stare and an icy shrug are the arctic reception for this quite modest request. 'Those are the hat bands... sir.' Exit one dissatisfied customer, still without a hat.

Now we come to the second shop and the no-problem man. 'You want a hat? Certainly sir, a bowler? Boater? Topper? Trilby? Deer-stalker? A trilby... quite so sir. They're not on display, but just one moment... and here they come. No problem.' The hats are produced. 'The colour is too light? Just so, sir. No problem. We do have other shades. Yes, here are some in a darker grey. Now that looks just about right. The hat band? The wrong colour? No problem sir,' He whisks open a drawer, momentarily displaying a kaleidoscope of colours, offers four for sir to choose from and has one temporarily in place so that sir can admire the effect for himself. All this in what appears to be three seconds flat. No problem. He makes the sale and sends a very satisfied customer out of the shop. A customer who is very likely to come back if he ever again needs something in the hat line.

The no-problem man. Of course there never really was a problem—other than the inevitable problem produced by a bored, lazy, uninterested and unco-operative, self-centred salesman. Not a real problem to which there seems to be no solution. Nothing like those geometry problems they used to give us at school where it seemed they never gave us enough information to enable us to work the thing out. Actually hospitality rarely presents *problems*. But hospitality does test our willingness to be hospitable. Hospitality demands the kind of person who positively enjoys giving it. The no-problem person is the one you want to be responsible for hospitality for the house group.

The no-problem person won't be tempted to do more

than is really necessary for the occasion; won't be mentally competing against the other women in the house group or what someone else in the church might have organized. No screams of horror at the thought of some late-comer having to sit on the floor, although a thoughtful cushion is a kindly act. No lakes of cream and fields of strawberries for some poor unfortunate to drop all over the new carpet, although I think tea or coffee, or whatever is appropriate, is a most enjoyable part of any house group meeting.

The hospitality leader should not only attend to chairs and refreshments, but should also be responsible to see that anything else needed for the meeting is at hand. Some house groups use a flip-pad, for writing up prayer requests or even for study outlines, which is very useful. It usually comes with a stand and a felt-tipped pen. This is more practical than a blackboard with all the mess that chalk dust produces in the home.

One other thing. The *home* that is used for house group meetings is very important. Not the house, but the home. It's very uncomfortable for everyone if husband and wife nag each other, or if the children are very demanding, or if there are dogs climbing all over everybody. On the other hand it's lovely to be in a home where husband and wife work together loyally, and make up one another's deficiencies without drawing attention to them.

I mean, it's awfully embarrassing if she spills the coffee and he rushes out for a cloth to clean up the resulting mess, and announces cheerfully to everyone, 'Oh, she's always doing that—she's like a bull in a china shop—hopeless, really....'

In a real sense most hospitality leadership is a joint affair. Husband, wife and children. If the house group is to relax, then you want a relaxed household—although not too relaxed. Make sure the room has adequate ventilation.

The prayer leader

The house group is an excellent setting for prayer. It's small enough for people to feel they don't have to make formal speeches or offer up artistic prayers. And since the house group quickly becomes a friendship group, people rapidly get to know one another and pray from knowledge and concern. This is real prayer.

In the churches this matter of prayer tends to be very poorly understood, very poorly presented and often not explained at all. The vicar or minister does most of it and the rest of us say amen at the end. We're not often prepared for prayer by being told just what we will be praying about and what we will be asking God to do through our prayers. This means we're praying for Jimmy Spicer although we have no idea what has happened to him. The minister is asking for 'a speedy recovery' as though Jimmy were a broken-down Ford Escort that the AA is going to bring in.

If the house group is going to do any better than this it will certainly need some help. Information first. Leaders tend to assume that everyone knows as much about the prayer items as they do, and everyone in the house group then assumes that since the leader isn't giving any information everyone else must have details already. So the group is unable to pray intelligently, simply because it doesn't have those necessary facts that make intelligent prayer possible. The group needs information.

Who is Jimmy Spicer? What happened to him? When? You want us to pray for Mr Tittlemarsh? Who is he? The chap who always sits at the end of the third row? Very tall. Has two kids and the teenager, Jill. She usually sits with him. What happened? Last Wednesday? Left her bag on the counter and when she remembered and went back for it it was gone. It wasn't just the money in it, but her car keys and, worst of all, her address book. She's lost without that. Yes, she's got another set of car keys, but she really needs that address book. So now *what* are we praying for? This is very important, so perhaps we'd better have a new paragraph.

What should we pray for? How are we to pray? I'm sure it would save a lot of frustration, disappointment and double-thinking if we studied this question very carefully. We are told in the Bible that if we ask for anything 'in the name of Jesus' our requests will be granted (Jn 14:14). But that does *not* mean we only have to tack the phrase 'in Jesus' name' on the end of our prayers to ensure that we will get whatever we've asked for. I say that so definitely because we all know from experience that that's not how prayer works. We've asked for something 'in the name of Jesus' and it hasn't been granted. So then what did Jesus mean when he said to ask 'in his name'.

It means *asking as Jesus would ask*. For example, Jesus also talked about 'giving a cup of water in my name' (Mk 9:41). He didn't mean giving someone a drink of water and adding the phrase 'in the name of Jesus'. He meant giving a cup of water as he would have given it. Jesus would look at the person, take an interest in him, say something to him, show that he was interested in him as a real and important person. I used to impress that on our missionaries when they came out to Africa. I told them, 'You'll meet beggars, people who are desperately poor, and I hope you'll be prepared to give them something. But when you do so, don't just throw them a coin and walk on. Always say something, as Jesus would have done.'

Doing anything 'in the name of' someone means doing it as that someone would have done it. Now let's apply that to prayer. How would Jesus pray? Firstly he would pray knowing about the matter he was praying for. Not blindly, or ignorantly. He would know. Secondly, Jesus would pray not for what he wanted, but for what his Father wanted. He would want the will of God to be carried through. Thirdly, because that was always the way

Jesus lived, in the will of his Father, he would have prayed knowing what his Father wanted to do. There would have been nothing in Jesus' own life that would have prevented him from knowing his Father's will.

It's this third area which demands much thought from us. Before we start to pray about Jimmy Spicer's recovery we need a kind of preliminary prayer, a prayer to find out what God actually wants to do in this case. And then we can confidently ask God to go ahead and do it.

I was once the minister of a church in Addis Ababa. Just before the evening service one Sunday, a message reached me to say that a young fellow I knew was missing. He was learning to fly and he had taken off for a lesson that afternoon, but the plane had not returned. Because the fuel would have been used up by now, it had to be down somewhere. The wild mountainous terrain of Ethiopia made the prospects poor. Would the church pray for his safety?

There were two ways open to me: to go into the church and pray a 'thy will be done' or an 'if it is thy will' prayer; or—the second possibility—to ask God to show me what he was going to do, and then pray definitely for that. So, as usual, I left someone else leading the service while I walked up and down outside the church, asking God to show me what he was going to do so that I would then know how to pray. Just before it was time for me to go in to preach, the answer was made quite clear to me. The lad was safe. I knew it. So I went in, told the congregation of the situation and led them in prayer, claiming the lad's safety. And then I carried on with the sermon. Half way through the sermon one of the congregation was called out to the telephone, and returned with a message which he brought up to me at the front of the church. The plane *had* crashed, but both occupants were safe. We sang the doxology!

Prayer leadership is a big responsibility. It requires someone who *prays*, not merely someone who knows about prayer. It requires a person of faith. It's not just a matter of mechanically assembling a prayer list and writing the requests up. It may well mean a good deal of preliminary praying, prayer that seeks to know God's will, and in faith sharing that knowledge with the house group. And so leading the house group into the marvellous experience of confident prayer.

Of course there *are* times when we simply can't discern what God's will is. This may be because natural human affection won't allow us to think of someone we love being taken from us—even though we know there comes a time for each of us to die. Or there may be an understandable shrinking away from a painful or difficult task. At such times it's good to admit, 'I just don't know how to pray, what to ask for, in this situation,' and to submit the whole issue to God and leave it there, with him—without any demands. And again we know it is always right to pray that God's people will still enjoy his peace and know his love in their difficulties. There's no need to ask, 'Is this what God wills in this instance?' It is!

On a practical level, the prayer leader should write up the prayer requests on the flip-pad, if the group has one, or any large sheet of paper will do. If you are planning on a fairly lengthy prayer time it's a good thing to divide the time into two or three sessions. This is especially helpful if some of the people in the group are not used to prayer.

Encourage everybody to open their eyes during the prayer session to remind themselves of the prayer requests or the names of the people who have been mentioned.

Some people do find this business of praying, even in a house group, quite unnerving. Such people can often be helped by being encouraged to write out a prayer before they come to the meeting, and then, during the prayer session, to read it. Those Christians who are accustomed to extempore prayer must be very careful here not to criticize the written prayer as though it were somehow second class.

The study leader

Notice this heading is *not* 'the speaker'. In fact that's just what you don't want of a study leader of a house group, a person who does all the talking. The right place for him is in the G3 large group. The value of the house group is that it makes it possible for everyone to take part. We can all chip in, ask our questions, offer our comments, suggest some answers. So the study leader is definitely not 'the speaker'. Very often the minister is the worst possible study leader. He may be so accustomed to talking without interruption that he will expect to do so in the house group. Even lay preachers may be a problem. And lecturers from theological colleges, too. They all know too much. If they just pour out all their wisdom, the rest of us may begin to feel very much like third-class passengers.

Well then, let's look at the study leader and try to find out what his task is. We should then be able to see what kind of person he needs to be.

His first task is to see that the group reaches its goal for the evening. The study leader knows what the group is supposed to be doing and he has to see that they do it. And that does mean keeping everybody to the point—in a sensible and flexible way. Not too many funny jokes. Not too many lengthy 'I remembers'. To keep Janet Hobby off her hobby horse—or at least to make sure that the ride is fairly short.

He will also have some part to play in assessing the house group afterwards: how did it go? Did we reach the goal? This task would almost certainly be shared with someone else though. We are often not very dispassionate judges of how we ourselves perform. Some of us always give ourselves an A, while others just as consistently assume failure. Still, it's not at all a bad thing for the study leader to try to produce an assessment of the house group meeting.

His second task is to see that everyone who wants to

take part does so. The first part of this task consists in keeping a careful check on just how much he himself does. He may well forget all the rules and use all the time himself. I was amused recently when a leader actually spoke for forty minutes, dismissed any kind of question time by inviting folks with questions to stay behind and have a chat afterwards, and then moved directly to the prayer slot with the injunction 'Keep your prayers short so that everyone can take part'!

Actually, the duty of the study leader is a bit more than merely ensuring that everyone who wants to take part does so. In a careful sort of way he should also ensure that everyone who *should* take part does so. Some of the house group may need a bit of encouragement. It's amazing to discover just how many Christians undervalue themselves. So many are convinced that what they have to say can't possibly be of any value. The study leader may well need to remind people that the Holy Spirit is in every one of them, revealing truth to them. Here is a factor that the 'professional' must never lose sight of: that the newest believer has the Holy Spirit in him, leading him to understand the truth. And he must remember that the new believer may well be more open to the truth than the long established believer who may feel he knows it all already.

Of course, what the study leader encourages is not merely a flow of answers, but also a steady flow of comments and questions. He will keep an eye on the members of the house group, and will be quick to spot the furrowed brow or to hear a muttered comment that needs to be brought out into the open.

This leads on to a third and very important task for the study leader: to protect those who take part. It is his responsibility to see that everyone feels secure, and knows that if they do take part then no one will make fun of them, belittle them, or sneer at them. The study leader does this *not* by waiting for someone to say something unkind and then jumping in like Giant Haystacks, but by setting a positive example. Every time a comment is made, a question asked, the study leader extracts from it everything that is good and helpful. The rest will soon pick up the good example, just as they would pick up a bad example of sarcasm or whatever.

Adults hate being made to look stupid in public. Once they know that what they have to say will be listened to carefully, with no funny remarks made at their expense (especially concerning their accent or grammar) they will take part and enjoy themselves. Otherwise they will simply clam up.

The fourth task of the study leader is to protect the house group from misinformation. This particular responsibility implies two things: firstly a willingness actually to do some study, and secondly to be able to drop in the necessary correction at the right moment and in the right way. What it does *not* imply is infallibility. The study leader must not imagine that he alone knows all the right answers (sometimes there *aren't* any *right* answers), that he is infallible—stating the question and supplying the authoritative answer all in the same breath. But this task does demand that the study leader engages in study.

I recall one church that was setting up house groups for the first time and they came to me for advice. One of the first things I asked about was how they proposed to *train* their study leaders. Oh, they wouldn't be training them. These people were much too busy to be able to give any of their valuable time to a training session. I'm afraid I had to suggest that in that case they had chosen the wrong people as study leaders, and must either find people who would do some study or else give up the idea of having house groups that did any study.

Of course the danger here is that ignorance is bliss. When you don't know how little you know, you may think that you know much more than you do. If you see what I mean. It's the person who reads and studies who actually knows that he doesn't know very much. That particular piece of knowledge, the knowledge that one is comparatively ignorant, is what makes a good, humble teacher.

Every church that sets up a system of house groups which are intended as study groups simply *must* set up along with it a system for training the study leaders. The training system will mean going through the study subject and the study materials together, with someone who really knows a bit about the subject and can anticipate the kind of questions that are likely to be asked. He can then indicate the general lines along which the questions should be approached.

The system may be very simple, consisting of a meeting each month where materials are presented, any perceived 'hot-spots' explained, followed by a discussion which enables the study leaders to get their questions answered, and perhaps concluding with a time of prayer. Or something more comprehensive might be attempted.

For example, I know of one church where the study sequence *begins* with a planning session at which the vicar discusses with a small advisory group *plus* the study leaders an agreed subject. Let's say it's the subject of divorce. The vicar will probably know the teaching and practice of the church and the general lines of biblical teaching. What he may not know are the particular sensitivities of the church members. Maybe there is someone attending church who was divorced before becoming a Christian, or someone whose parents have recently been divorced. Unfeeling and academic discussion of matters which in fact could be deeply painful to some people is something to be avoided.

There should certainly be no assumption that the vicar alone knows all about the subject. A team approach is very important. The team's feelings then feed into the following Sunday's preaching which is a means of directing the congregation's thinking towards the month's topic, and of giving some basic teaching. And, perhaps, of raising a few questions in the minds of the congregation, questions that will re-appear in the house groups.

In the following week the same subject is on the agenda of whatever age groups or interest groups the church may have, and these in turn feed into the house group meetings in the third week. So back to the next planning session, where the whole exercise can be evaluated and a bit of fine tuning done in preparation for the next occasion when the subject will be tackled.

Yes, it takes a good deal of time and effort, but the church feels the benefit, right enough. And the vicar is one of the first to express his appreciation of the learning process that he goes through each time the advisory group meets.

The fifth task of the study leader is to keep the programme moving. He should have a fair idea of how much time is allocated to each part of the evening's meeting, and should ensure that the group keeps to it, more or less. 'More or less', because it is *very* unwise to try to insist on the group ending a discussion they want to continue. The leader may get his own way if he forces the closure, but the group won't love him for it! He could find himself with a smouldering revolt on his hands. And the study leader might as well realize from the very beginning that he is entirely dependent on the willing co-operation of the group. If they rebel, he can't keep them in after school, or make them write out five hundred lines....

However, provided the job is tactfully done, most groups are only too grateful to have a leader who will rescue them from a protracted discussion—especially one that is getting nowhere—and will keep the evening's programme flowing.

One helpful way of ensuring that the programme does flow is the use of *chunking*. There will be more about chunking in a later chapter, but it deserves a mention here. Chunking is simply dividing the evening up into chunks, so ensuring reasonable variety. So much time for coffee, so much time for Bible reading. So much time for introducing the subject. Discussion due to start at such and such a time. So much time to be reserved for prayer. The study leader should have a note in front of him, telling him when each new chunk of time should begin, so that he can more or less keep to it.

The final task of the study leader is to act as a kind of referee when disagreements occur. Again, we'll talk about this side of house group management in a later chapter, and at greater length, but it is vital to ensure that disagreements are not merely swept under the carpet. In fact it's very often the disagreements that are the most effective teaching and learning experiences. People remember the things they have argued about, because they argue about the things they feel most deeply about. The study leader should realize disagreements are not necessarily a bad thing.

The Study Leader and His Responsibilities

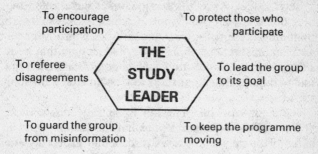

To encourage
participation

To protect those who
participate

**THE
STUDY
LEADER**

To referee
disagreements

To lead the group
to its goal

To guard the group
from misinformation

To keep the programme
moving

But a disagreement will only be of value to the group if it is handled in the right way. Obviously the disagreement itself needs to be expressed in a Christian way. The study leader may need to take the heat out of one statement, an implied sting out of another, or to rephrase a disagreement more tactfully, more *Christianly*.

When things do get hot there is one very effective way of bringing people back to rational, humble Christian attitudes again: prayer. When tempers are getting frayed simply call for two or three minutes of prayer. Maybe ask two people to lead the whole group in appropriate prayer, asking for whatever is missing in the debate: patience, grace, openness or whatever. But a word of caution: beware of letting the main protagonists lead the prayer. There are few things more odious than one person using prayer in order to get back at another.

After prayer, the group will usually find that the discussion can be continued, but in a more Christian tone of voice.

*   *   *

Bearing in mind these tasks to be performed by the study leader, the church should be in a position to choose house group leaders. And the church should also be able to see that there is very much more to effective house groups than merely chopping up the congregation into six groups and sending them off to six homes to do some Bible study. Leadership of the groups is a vital matter: the right hospitality leaders, the right prayer leaders and the right study leaders.

If the groups are successful, you may well discover before very long that you need another leader: someone to co-ordinate the pastoral care of the group. As the group matures and the members gain confidence, the group is likely to grow and to identify fresh tasks that it might wish to take on. Among those tasks pastoral care is almost certain to have high priority. Members of the house group will minister to one another. There will be a growing concern that no member of the house group should have a need that is overlooked. So a fourth member of the leadership team emerges, the pastoral leader.

Shared Leadership in the House Group

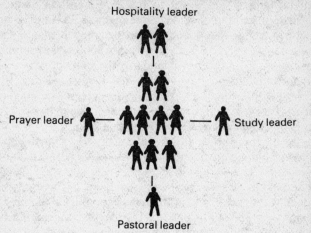

Hospitality leader

Prayer leader

Study leader

Pastoral leader

Now can you see how all this fits in with the idea that in a church each member has something to contribute? Not all the gifts are concentrated in one person, the minister. Rather they are spread by the Holy Spirit throughout the church membership.

Supposing the church has six house groups, you might well have twenty-four people involved in leadership tasks for which they have actually been gifted by the Spirit. There is no reason why any one of the twenty-four should be part of the leadership team that has already been set up in the church. *Everyone* in the church is gifted (1 Cor 12:7), and house groups present the church with a clear means of putting the gifts to work.

People in the house group couldn't perhaps cope with major leadership responsibilities for the whole church. Elders, deacons, vicars and ministers might well feel engulfed by taking on yet one more leadership responsibility. In fact house groups should lead to a more biblical pattern of church life, a more effective learning programme and a more satisfying pattern of pastoral care.

CHAPTER 5

But What Do We Teach?

The answer to this question is made up of three parts: teach what the people in the house group need to know; teach what the study leader is capable of teaching; teach some part of the church's Education Programme.

Teach what is needed

We need to teach what the people in the house group need to know. This is such an obvious principle, yet somehow very few churches seem to take it seriously.

Just consider our marvellous choice of evening classes in Britain. What is on offer? Here in front of me lies a local leaflet entitled *Adult Leisure Classes*. The leaflet tells me I can learn to paint houses or pictures, to type or to take photographs. I can study dressmaking, cookery or gardening. I can learn to make furniture, repair cars and how to use a computer. All the things that ordinary people want to learn. But offer the average man a two-year course in eleventh-century metaphysics and he'll think you're joking. In any event he won't take you up on your offer, because he can't see what use such a course could be to him and the subject doesn't grab him. Eleventh-century metaphysics doesn't even *sound* interesting to Mr Average

Man. Now those are the two main reasons people give for studying something. Either they feel they can *use* the knowledge they gain or they find the subject interesting in itself, even if it can't actually be used in any way.

These are the two factors which need bearing in mind as we plan what to teach in our house groups. But it becomes immediately obvious that we are likely to find that what is valuable for *this* house group doesn't much interest *that* house group. The people in the two groups are different. No problem. Accept that. Don't try to *make* people study something that simply doesn't interest them. Instead, allow for flexibility on certain subjects, taking careful note of what study leaders or hospitality leaders advise regarding suitable topics for *their* groups.

So then, before attempting to set out in cold print what you expect the grand plan of study for the house groups to be, spend some time in finding out what they need to know so they can *use* the knowledge, and what they want to know simply because it interests them. There will be more about this grand plan in the third part of this chapter.

Teach what you can

Secondly, then, *teach what the study leader is capable of teaching*. It's no good trying to teach archaeology (even if the group *wants* to study the subject) if there isn't anyone in the group who knows anything about archaeology. Here I'm widening up the possibilities for study leadership. We must get away from the idea that the study leader, once appointed, will be the study leader of the house group no matter what. It would very much surprise me if from time to time there wasn't someone else in the house group who could handle the night's subject better than the usual study leader. If the study leader is not married it would be very odd to ask him to lead a study on the Christian family. If there happened to be a solicitor in the group then he should be able to tackle any studies bearing on law. Of course he might have to do a bit of reading up on the biblical side, but he would probably get far more out of it than the usual study leader, also having to do some study of the biblical side, but without the advantage of a legal background. A doctor might handle questions of medical ethics, a postman might lead a discussion on the Christian at work, a nurse could talk about the problem of pain as *she* saw it.

Obviously if the group is stuck with the idea of just *one* study leader they will be impoverished; there will be many subjects that he will know himself to be unqualified to say anything about at all. Occasional changes in the leadership of the group are good for everyone. However, teach what the study leader is capable of teaching.

Now thirdly. And this is the major part of this chapter. The house group should get teaching that is some part of the church's Education Programme.

The Church Education Programme

We saw in chapter two that Jesus told his followers they were to *teach*. In turn, Paul taught Timothy, and told him to pass on what he had learned to other men who would be able to teach others as well (2 Tim 2:2). The fact is that Christianity is more than going to church. We have to study our faith so that we will be able to teach our children and answer the kinds of questions that the people we work with and the neighbours are likely to ask. We also need to study so that we will be able to answer our own questions. We all of us go through times when things seem to go wrong and Christianity doesn't appear to add up. At those times it's the Christian who has studied his faith who finds himself able to answer his questions, settle his doubts. The instructed Christian can cope and cope *triumphantly* in such times.

The church needs a carefully thought out programme of

education for its members so that they will develop and become mature Christians. But what are the principles of education? Here are four characteristics of genuine programmes of education.

1. Education is progressive

Today's lessons follow on from yesterday's. There's a pattern in the scheme of teaching that is partly due to the fact that some parts of learning are more difficult than other parts, and can't be tackled until the easier bits have been mastered. Mathematics is an obvious example. You learn arithmetic first and then algebra. You learn addition first and then multiplication. What you don't do is learn advanced mathematics and then go back to simple addition. Or go on learning simple addition year after year.

Actually, you can see this principle of progressive education in Hebrews 6 —

> Therefore let us leave the elementary teachings about Christ and go on to maturity (1)

and again in 1 Corinthians 3:

> Brothers, I could not address you as spiritual but as worldly— mere infants in Christ. I gave you milk, not solid food, for you were not yet ready for it. Indeed, you are still not ready (vv 1–2).

All sensible study programmes observe this principle of progressive teaching—teaching that builds on what was learned at some earlier stage.

In school this is a comparatively easy matter. First of all we can tell roughly what any child knows simply by finding out his age. A child of six hasn't yet started on eleventh-century metaphysics, for example! In church things aren't quite so easy. One person may have been a Christian for thirty years and yet scarcely know the Old Testament from the New. Another person may have been a Christian for only two years but have a degree in theology. So it *is* difficult to sort out the confusion but it is important to try to do it, and to see that new Christians get the basics and that mature Christians aren't kept on the same old diet of basics when they'd really like to get on a bit further.

It then follows that house groups are the wrong place for teaching the basics. Since they normally represent the whole spectrum of the church, young and old, new believers and mature Christians, the basics would only be appropriate in very rare situations. Where everyone was a new Christian, for example, or where no one had ever heard the basics explained before. But where a church has been going for some time and there has at least been some good teaching given, it is best to arrange separate classes (nurture groups, they are sometimes called, though I find the label a bit patronizing) for new Christians, held at regular intervals and into which all new believers are automatically channelled. They should then get a kind of crash course, or a course of accelerated teaching, that will enable them to fit into the house groups which are teaching stuff that's a bit further down the line.

2. Education is student orientated

Students are given what they actually need to know. This ensures that teaching is relevant and that, in turn, at least encourages the students to co-operate with the teachers. What is more, this relevance is related to the current situation of the student. You'll have noticed that in our schools education becomes more and more specialized as the years go by. Everybody needs to know the basics of a whole range of subjects, so in the early years children learn English and arithmetic and history and art and biology and geography and... an almost endless list of different subjects.

But then the education programme becomes more restricted. The children have the basics for the further study of almost everything, and so they begin to narrow down their studies: maybe six or seven O-levels or CSEs. Further narrowed down to three A-levels. And maybe just geography at university. At each level the student is given just what is necessary for his particular needs. Doctors aren't expected to study early church history. Scientists aren't expected to read Chaucer. The people who design the courses are all concerned to ensure that students learn everything they need to learn, but don't waste time learning things that are just not necessary.

In the same way, the church needs to ask itself very seriously: 'What do the people who come to this church need to learn?' We can find the answers to this question in the same way as the people at the universities do about what doctors or engineers have to learn. We must find out what our students are expected to be able to *do*.

So instead of asking, 'What must the Christians in our church learn?' let's use a different question: 'What must the Christians in our church be able to do?' We can produce a list fairly easily:

* They must be able to live in a Christian way at home.
So: they must understand the Christian ideal of marriage
     they must know something about the Christian way of bringing up their children
     they must be able to answer the kinds of question that their children are likely to ask
     they must be able to develop a good relationship with their neighbours
     they must learn about the value of family prayers and how to arrange them

* They must be able to live in a Christian way at work.
So: they must understand something of the Christian attitude to work
     they must be able to answer the kind of questions that are likely to be asked by the others at work

they must know something about the Christian attitude to Trade Unions and strike action

* They must be able to enjoy life at the church.
So: they must learn about the Communion service and other special church services

they must learn about the Bible and why it is given such an important place in the church

they must learn about prayer: how it works, what it is

they must learn about God: who he is, how he reveals himself, how we should relate to him

* They must be able to cope with accident, illness and death.
So: they must learn about the problem of human suffering and how they can still believe in a loving God despite it

they must learn the Christian doctrine of death

they must know about heaven, hell and judgement

The list could be made much longer, but if we take teaching seriously we will need a programme of teaching that will enable Christians to do these things.

And don't forget that this list only includes the subjects that Christians ought to learn because they are useful, because the Christian can actually do something with his knowledge. A place must also be found for teaching some things which the people at the church want to learn about even if the knowledge can't immediately be put to work.

So the teaching programme is student orientated. It's worth emphasizing here that the teaching is, therefore, not *teacher* orientated. In general, teachers aren't free to teach only the things that happen to interest them. They have some kind of syllabus to follow, a syllabus that was probably put together by someone else in a way that reflected the needs of the students. The teacher can't throw that all away and teach something different just because the something different interests *him*.

I learned that the hard way when I was a teacher at a Royal Air Force Technical Training School. I was supposed to be teaching electricity, but the syllabus was really rather dull. I enjoyed teaching electricity, but not *these* bits of the subject; what I enjoyed was complicated electrical circuits and working out the currents flowing in each of the arms of the circuits. So I abandoned the syllabus and got the men on to electrical circuits and something called Kirchoff's Laws, and we all had a great time. I was enjoying myself, the men caught my enthusiasm and were enjoying themselves, and all was happiness and light. Then, in walked the school's Commanding Officer. There was no way of hiding what I was doing. The blackboard was covered with beautiful diagrams of electrical circuits and mathematical calculations. There was a stony silence. The Commanding Officer walked round inspecting the note books. That told him just how long this had all been going on. Mind you, the men had *learned* something. And they had *enjoyed* learning it. And it *was* 'electricity'. But it wasn't what the syllabus said they needed to learn. A few questions were followed by an invitation to the CO's office. Ouch! It was made very clear to me that I wasn't there to enjoy myself, but to teach the men what they needed to know. If I enjoyed it so much the better, but the syllabus and the needs of the men were the things I was to remember. It was a good lesson to learn, and in more than thirty years I've not forgotten it.

Ministers please note.

3. Teaching should be active not passive

Teachers have at last learned that it is *not* a good thing to train the children to sit still with their arms folded while information is poured down their throats like a dose of salts. In school the children are expected to take part in class sessions: to ask questions as well as to try to answer them.

Children are involved in actually finding out information for themselves. They get involved in drama, role play.

There is a real sense in which the boundary line between teacher and taught has become blurred: both are teaching and both are learning. Teachers take this matter of participation seriously, so when they write to those of us who are parents and complain that our children must learn to participate more in class activities, it's not just a peculiar fad of the teacher. The concern arises from the fact that the teacher knows active participation is invaluable to the whole learning process.

In church we have tended to take a different view. We look on silence from the congregation as being golden. I recall speaking once at a mid-week service somewhere. Half way through my talk I was rewarded with a question. I was delighted. Someone was listening! But afterwards one of the elders from the church came to me to apologize for the interruption....

4. Teaching today is normally multi-medial

Which means that the teacher does not spend all the lesson time just talking. He will use the blackboard, he may use a film, a sound-strip, models, drama, debate. The teacher is concerned to bring variety into the classroom.

This is not merely because variety is the spice of life. It is because the teaching process somehow has to cope with what is called the *attention span*. The attention span represents the length of time that a person can go on doing something without losing concentration. Quite obviously the length of my attention span depends on what that something is. But no matter what it is I will eventually come to the end of my attention span for it, and I will want to do something different. My mind will wander.

Mind you, our minds will wander anyway. We keep switching off every few minutes, so that we can think over, sort out and organize the new things we've been hearing. Maybe you've noticed that? You're listening to a really good and interesting talk but you suddenly realize you've lost the drift of what the speaker is saying. What has happened is simple. The speaker has said something particularly interesting and relevant, or perhaps a little bit difficult to take in, and you have switched off any more input so your mind can get to work, teasing out that one important, interesting bit of information. Ah! *Now* I see! And you switch back on again. But you've missed a couple of minutes of the talk, probably without even noticing it. This process of switching on and off is automatic, instinctive, and it explains why we lose the drift, even of a good talk. (And, incidentally, it explains why it's not a good idea to develop ideas in *long* complicated stretches of speech. Or if you do, then it's important to put in summaries every so often, to help those who have had to switch off to plug back in again.)

However, this *attention span* matter is something quite different. Even if a speaker is very good, and even if you can understand what he is saying and don't need to switch off, in fact, if he goes on too long, you will come to the end of your attention span and simply be unable to take in any more. The speaker has gone on too long.

But how long is 'too long'? The length of your attention span depends on dozens of factors, but on five factors in particular:

1. The subject being talked about. If the subject interests you then your attention span is longer than for a subject which bores you.
2. The speaker—especially the speakers's voice. If it is an attractive voice, and clearly audible then the attention span is longer than for a person with a thin, monotonous voice.
3. The difficulty of the subject. Now that is determined far more by the speaker than by the subject. An interesting speaker can make a potentially difficult subject simple and a poorly organized speaker can make a simple subject seem like something on a level with Einstein.
4. The circumstances. The attention span depends a little

bit on other things that compete for attention. An uncomfortable chair soon demands attention. A very hot room does. So does someone in the next chair who is playing noughts and crosses. What we call 'distraction' is simply the normal human situation, where several matters are competing for attention at the same time.
5. The way in which the information is presented.

Obviously what we want to do when we teach is to ensure the longest possible attention span. The subject is fixed: someone has decided that this group of people needs to study this subject. I'm the speaker and I probably can't do too much with my voice—although you can do more than you think. At least you can speak loudly enough. And not like an express train. And you might try listening to yourself via a tape recorder. The difficulty of the subject can be reduced by a determined effort on my part to understand it myself, first, before I presume to try to teach someone else. Here's a worthwhile principle: to be able to explain something *simply* you must understand it *profoundly*. So I can help to make the subject more easily understood by making sure that I understand it. And then I can probably do something about the circumstances—or at least the hospitality leader of the house group can do something.

But note that fifth point: the attention span of my audience will depend to some extent on the way in which the information is presented. If it's all talk the attention span may be quite brief. And that is very difficult for ministers to accept. Preachers tend to assume that their congregations have got the same length attention span as they themselves have. But that's largely wishful thinking. Preachers go to theological colleges. Theological colleges tend to be reactionary sorts of institutions, where the main emphasis is still on fifty-minute lectures. Preachers get that for three years. After three years they're a bit like Pavlov's dogs, conditioned to respond to end-of-lesson warning bells after fifty minutes. They are trained, like circus lions, to sit for fifty minutes on uncomfortable seats... and even to make what they optimistically refer to as notes. But most of the congregation hasn't been conditioned like that. For them it's watching TV that does the conditioning. Watch the programme, get up and change channels, look at the *TV Times*, go and make a quick cup of tea, here come the adverts, another five minutes. It's all neatly chunked, and it all indicates a very short attention span.

But the attention span can be lengthened if we will only change the way in which we're doing things. Read a bit from the Bible (no, not you: someone else, a new voice), ask a question, point the place out on a map. Use a tape recorder to play back something relevant: a current song, an extract from a cassette bought at one of the Bible Conventions. Even make use of a video: there are plenty of good Christian videos on the market now, and it's almost as easy to show a video in the home as it is to use a tape recorder.

Schools make use of combinations of all these possibilities, and we must learn to do the same. The best education is multi-medial, and multiplying the media expands the attention span.

So, there are four basic principles of an effective education programme. The task of the church is to make effective use of every teaching activity and somehow make them all contribute to the total programme. This should mean that the Sunday School, Bible classes (especially if the church has managed to introduce some kind of all-age Bible class system), Crusader classes, YP sessions, men's meetings, women's meetings, deacons' meetings, meetings of the Parochial Church Council (which should *not* be suffered to remain a mere committee meeting but be used for training), and the house groups all have a deliberately assigned role in the CEP. And as the package is put together, and training sessions held, the four principles will be kept firmly in mind.

Finding out what to teach

The answer to the problem of knowing what to teach appears quite simple: ask the people themselves. But there is a catch to it. If the vicar asks his congregation for their suggestions it will inevitably be a certain few who will come up with anything. The 'second coming' brigade want Daniel and Revelation. The 'charismatics' want prophecy and healing. The 'progressives' want women in the church and the simple style of living. Now whether any of them really need what they want is quite a question. For them the menu is easily defined and comparatively concise.

Another problem, however, is that most people in the church, when asked for their suggestions regarding a teaching diet, won't have the least idea of what's on the menu. Some kind of preliminary instruction is needed before most Christians can get the idea of the vast possible scope of a CEP.

But there again, you can't ask the church leaders to write down a list of what ought to be taught, because they probably come out of the social top-drawer, while the majority of the congregation are rather less so.

One way of getting a *reasonable* sort of list is to circulate to everyone in the church a very long list of possible subjects to be studied. It's best to distribute the list before a church service and then give time to ticking off preferences at some appropriate spot in the service. Have the lists handed in during the service. That method guarantees an almost one hundred percent response. With a one hundred percent response you can be fairly confident that an analysis will yield a reasonable idea of what people want.

However, the real proof of the pudding is in the eating.

If you lay on a series of studies and no one turns up, then there's something wrong either with the teacher, or with the subject *even if everyone in the church voted for it*. Unfortunately when people make suggestions for a teaching programme they are merely suggesting, as intelligent people, what in their opinion such a programme should contain, without any commitment whatsoever to attend the courses. This is illustrated neatly in an account I read of an agency that was marketing handbags. What colour would be most popular? To find out they put together a panel of ladies, sat them down at desks, gave each a form on which they had to indicate which colour they preferred: red, green, black, or brown. The papers were collected up and then the organizer spoke. He thanked the ladies for their co-operation, and then offered them a free gift as a token of appreciation. It was one of the handbags. There were four tables set up near the exit, one with red handbags, one with green handbags, one with black and one with brown. All they had to do was take one as they left. The ladies were gratified and duly took one each. The first noticeable factor was that there was very little correlation between what they had written on their forms and what they actually took. The second thing to note was that the agency disregarded the forms. What they took notice of was what the ladies actually took.

So if people don't turn up, don't expect to discover the reason why by asking them. They may well assure you that they'd *love* to come. It's absolutely the right subject. But if they don't come, it probably isn't the right subject....

What Goes into the Christian Education Programme

BASIC COURSE or Nurture Group

THEOLOGICAL

The creed. God the Father. Who is Jesus?
The Holy Spirit. The Trinity. Creation. What
is man? Man's responsibility for God's
world. Sin: what it is and where it
comes from. Satan. Forgiveness,
Salvation and Christian behaviour.
Death, judgement, heaven
and hell. The Bible
and inspiration
Prayer

ETHICS

Marriage and
the family
Family planning
Divorce
Drugs, alcohol,
smoking
Gambling
The problem of
suffering
Crime and punish-
ment
Law and order
The place of
ambition
Rich Christians
and the poor
nations

OCCASIONAL

Genetic engineering
Glue sniffing
Surrogate motherhood
Liberation theology
Billy Graham
Capital punishment

CIVICS

The Christian and
the State
The Christian and
politics
The Christian and
war
The Christian as
employee and
employer
The Christian and
money

THE CHURCH

The birth of the church.
How the church functions:
ministry and organization.
The sacraments of the church.
The church and world mission;
mission societies.
Relationships with other churches:
orthodox, unorthodox.
Relationships with other religions
and with cults.

Yes, I know that there is
  an enormous amount of material outlined there
    but
      which bits would you leave out?
        and why?
          And actually that's not everything
            even now.
              I've left out
                Bible study itself
and that could keep you going for the whole of the year
without a break.
  But if Christians are to become mature
    they have to learn
      they have to learn what Christians believe
        so that they can say something
          SAY SOMETHING distinctively CHRISTIAN
            at work
              in the supermarket,
                or in the bus queue
                or at school.
                  Anywhere.
                    Everywhere.

Organizing the Church Education Programme

We don't usually make the most of the many 'meetings' held in the church each week. It is true that initially it takes a real effort to work out a sensible CEP for the church, but the effort is well repaid and the result is that each meeting contributes to the growth of the whole church. Of course there must be 'breathing space' built into the programme so that leaders of the various organizations can feel free to slot in special activities. But the teaching programme really should be part of the progressive and integrated teaching programme of the whole church.

So here's an example of a scheme that might be used as a kind of pattern for a church setting up a CEP for the first time. It assumes Sunday services, house groups and special meetings for men, women and the YP. (Incidentally it's worth remembering that there is a place for YP meetings where they split into fellows and girls: they *do* have separate problems which can best be handled by dividing up.) The scheme is only a suggestion. Use what you can, modify, adapt.

The scheme here covers just one month. Other months might well be spent in a very different pattern. It certainly is not intended that this four-week pattern should be repeated throughout the twelve months of the year.

The first week begins with a Family Service on the Sunday. As with all the main church sessions, a question box or two is available, prominently displayed, and people are encouraged to use it. One way of encouraging people to use a suggestions box is to refer to it when suggestions or questions from it are taken up by the church. That encourages folks to feel that something is actually done with their suggestions. If the church has two services or more in the day it is assumed here that one service will be for outreach. There will be a definite goal of getting outsiders in.

Still in the first week there is some kind of church gathering for prayer and for sharing. Prayer is particularly directed towards the imminent *training class*. As we've already seen, the training class involves the vicar, the house group leaders and any other folks who might be able to provide input. They share responsibility for planning the teaching of the month's set subject. The minister *learns* and does not merely teach.

The following Sunday in the sermon (and in the Sunday School, and especially in the adult 'Sunday School' if you have one) the new subject is presented. Let's say 'The Holy Spirit'. The theme might well be carried on in the evening service, taking care to do two things: to relate the subject to the part of the congregation that just comes to *this* service (for whatever reason) *and* to build on what was done in the morning service. No, those two aren't contradictory. One part of your congregation *can* be getting more out of a talk than another part—they can make connections that the others will be unaware of—and the speaker will not even have to refer to the connections. It flows out of careful preparation.

During the following week, the second week of the scheme, the same theme is carried through at the special meetings for men, women and young people. Their leaders were at the monthly training class, and know what their special contribution is to be. So by the end of the second week there has been a good deal of input and some people, at any rate, are beginning to ask questions. These can be picked up in the Sunday School classes, and any major issues presented in the sermon.

And now come the crucial house groups. The house group leaders have been participating in the various input sessions and have looked at the questions that have been sent in through the question boxes. So they are ready with a fairly limited new input, but prepared for discussion, dialogue, which should lead to genuine learning. And all this feeds in turn into the fourth Sunday's activities. And so to the meeting of the Church Education Programme Committee at which there is general discussion of how the teaching has been received, and how the system might be improved. And on again to the monthly training class.

Two comments should be made here. First of all, that we are surely wrong in separating teaching from evangelism. As Martyn Lloyd-Jones insisted in chapter 14 of his book *Preaching and Preachers* (Hodder & Stoughton), people are regularly saved through good solid Bible teaching. The second point is that it seems to me quite wrong that men's meetings, women's meetings, YP meetings and the Sunday School meetings should all go on without the leadership of the church having any hand at all in what is being taught. Frankly, the situation in most churches is sheer chaos. No one knows what's being done and what isn't being done. The fact is that from what I've seen in scores of churches most young people are *never* taught the things they need to know as young people and it's no wonder at all that so many young Christians are metaphorically knock-kneed and cross-eyed. It is sheer laziness on the part of the church's leaders that allows the situation to continue. Either that or the church leadership is so tied up with business matters that they have no time for the real task, which is not insuring the building but instructing the living stones.

It is obvious that in a big church it is impossible for one person to organize all that is needed for a successful CEP. Especially if the one person is an already over-worked vicar. But as a church gets bigger so, inevitably, the skills to be found in the congregation multiply. Most bigger churches attract some school teachers. Well, let's use their professional expertise in setting up a CEP.

What has been discussed here is just one of thousands of possible variations of a CEP. Notice that the CEP really focuses on the house groups, precisely because of what has been said all through this book, that it is in the house groups that the best learning is achieved. And yet house groups ought not to become isolated from the rest of church life. Integration multiplies effectiveness. So then, attempt to produce some level of integration by pulling out of this chapter those bits that directly apply to your situation, adapt what needs to be modified and use that, too. But only discard ideas with reluctance. And you may need to be brutally frank in explaining *why* 'it won't work here'.

CHAPTER 6

Have You Tried This?

I've already suggested that modern educational methods are very different from the old ones. But somehow these new methods, new ideas, take a very long time to filter into the churches. I suppose that at least part of the reason for this state of affairs is that until recently the churches were very much churches of elderly people. And older people usually resist new ideas. As a result, sermons are still largely 'talking heads' and small study groups turn out to be in reality little more than boiled down sermons. In their way sermons, like lectures, are all right as a means for teaching some things. But on the whole the lecture, or sermon, is probably the least efficient and one of the less effective ways of teaching.

And if you do manage to get a group of people together who are prepared to participate, it's a shame not to attempt other ways of teaching beside the talk/lecture/sermon.

One of the principal features of educational thinking, as we saw in the last chapter, concerns *participation*. Here are seven methods of running a house group meeting, all of them involving the group in some measure of participation.

Leader and led

The traditional way of handling a small group study. The method is very dependent, almost totally dependent, on the effectiveness of the leader. If he isn't much good then the study group won't be much good either. And if he is the type who talks too much then the house group will degenerate into a G3 group with too few members. People will become frustrated because although they feel they *ought* to be able to talk back and ask questions, no opportunity for doing it is given.

Of course if the study leader is a *very* good G3 leader the group may settle for that, and turn the house group into a house church!

Interrogation

This method doesn't take a great deal of preparation so far as the study leader is concerned, but does need careful timing to ensure that everyone goes away satisfied with what has been accomplished. It's very easy to leave without having got to the end of the programme.

So this is what happens. After, say, ten minutes of introduction the house group divides into two smaller groups. Each little group talks over the subject, examines the Bible passage, if there is one set, and prepares three genuine questions for the other group to consider. After fifteen or twenty minutes the two groups exchange their sets of questions, and spend the next twenty minutes trying to produce answers to one, or two, or perhaps even all three of their questions. And finally the two groups join together for a session in which all six questions are considered by both groups. Along with such answers as have been suggested.

Let's assume that the group is trying to answer the question of what happens to people who have never heard the gospel. The Bible passage to be studied is Romans 1.

Notice that it is better to set a whole chapter of the Bible rather than a single verse. This gives a reasonable assurance that the group will identify the context of the whole passage, and also gives the group enough material to form a base for a worthwhile study.

The study leader suggests a chapter division:

verses	1–7	Introduction
verses	8–17	An explanation of the reason for writing the letter
verses	18–32	Part one of a thorough analysis of the whole gospel, dealing particularly with God's response to human evil.

Now the house group divides up. Don't, however, encourage the groups to separate, one lot going out into the hall, or into another room. I find that the noisiness of a room in which two or more groups are working is helpful. It seems to provide people with a comforting sense of anonymity, a soothing background of noise, so that they don't feel they are making speeches into an intimidating silence.

They begin to study Romans 1. They might have a question to ask about Paul's proposition that people ought to be able to discern God simply by looking at the evidence of creation. For example:

'If people look around them at the world, at nature, aren't they just as likely to see evidence of cruelty, suffering, pain and disease, as they are evidence of a gracious God? So how would that fit in with verse 20?'

Meanwhile the other group might be asking:

'Surely verse 23 isn't true of everybody? Haven't *some* people looked at the world, found God, and worshipped him? So is Paul speaking about a general law applying to everyone, or is he only referring to some people at some point in history?'

Now that's all very gratifying. Two fascinating theological questions. And some house groups just might produce them. But not many. This kind of thinking is not the general way of thinking. It's sometimes labelled 'middle-class thinking' and associated with the middle-class learning mentality. The middle-class learning approach is through *propositions*. Nearly all higher level education is of this type. But beware of assuming that everyone thinks that way. They don't. Nor is the middle-class way either the only way or the best way of thinking. We must not demand that everyone in our house groups must think and learn the middle-class way.

The majority of people, the masses, don't think in terms of propositions or of abstract ideas. The masses will say: 'It isn't fair,' and, 'He didn't ought to do it,' and, 'Well, is it right?' and, 'Did it happen like it says or didn't it happen like that?' Notice the 'it' in there. A reference to an event. An accident, a theft, a lie told, an account of what happened last night. Not *propositional* thinking but *anecdotal* thinking. Most people prefer to think in concrete terms of things happening, of real life stories. Exactly the kind of story that Jesus used to tell. About people going to Jericho, and people sowing seeds, and people building houses.

Most people understand stories better than theories. And for that reason Romans 1 would not be a particularly good chapter for the average house group. In fact if Romans 1 is the typical sort of Bible passage chosen for study by the house group, the house group will steadily turn into a particular sort—a middle-class house group. Church members who don't enjoy, or don't understand, theories and propositions will stop coming to it.

I rather think that preachers this century have spent far too much time in Paul's letters and far too little time in the gospels and Acts. In the Old Testament, Genesis is particularly rich in family stories which are highly relevant today.

There are stories that should produce raised eyebrows and heated discussion. Try, for example, Genesis 22. Abraham offering—or nearly offering—his son Isaac as a sacrifice. And listen very carefully to the questions that are likely to be asked by non-theologians, but still thinking people, loving mothers and fathers, about that story.

Or instead of starting from a Bible passage, you might want to start from current affairs and move from that to the Bible. Start with famine in Asia and then talk about God's promise that harvests would continue throughout history (Gen 8:22). No, I'm not being cynical at all. There really is a Christian answer to the apparent contradiction highlighted here. And it's the kind of answer that Christians need to know. The theologians call this topic *theodicy*: defending God's character even in the face of human suffering. But don't announce 'theodicy' as your subject but rather, 'Does God produce famine?'

Tackle-a-problem

In this type of study we don't start from a verse of the Bible and talk about the meaning of the verse. Instead we start from some problem that Christians recognize, talk about the problem and see what answers the Bible might suggest.

Take the problem of war. Should Christians fight in a war? Is there, could there be, such a thing as a 'just war'? Was the Second World War a just war? Was that war an example of the kind of war in which a Christian could fight with a clear conscience. Think about the Nazi massacre of the Jews. Think about the atom bombs dropped on Hiroshima and Nagasaki. Should Christians take the line that all war, all violence, is wrong?

This problem-centred approach to an evening's study

opens up all sorts of possible new approaches. You could arrange for two members of the house group to prepare the two opposing viewpoints, and have a kind of debate. (Only don't push the debate to a vote. If you do that you might well find some people getting very upset. And there's a more important principle to be kept in mind: truth is not determined by a majority vote.)

Or another possibility. Ask the house group to divide into two: those who think fighting is always wrong, and those who think there could be occasions when it would be right to fight. Then ask each group to prepare and present the case for the other side. In other words, the pacifists present the view that it could be right to fight in certain circumstances, while the non-pacifists present the case for pacifism. Now that really is a soul-searching experience, but, surprisingly enough, most people tackle the task fairly and enjoy the Alice-through-the-looking-glass approach.

Drama

The difficulty with any kind of drama in the house group is that many folks, especially the older ones, are afraid of it—afraid of being asked to make fools of themselves in public. Where drama is used in church it's just people who *like* that sort of thing who are expected to get involved, but when drama moves into the small group maybe *I* could get caught up in it. Still, the house group is small, and provided that you have given time for everyone to get to know everyone else you should find that most people are willing to join in. And if someone really doesn't want to, don't push it.

Drama covers all sorts of activities. What's called 'role-play' is simply an attempt to think oneself into a particular type of character. There will be seven chunks in an evening given over to role-play:

1. Introduction by the study leader

His task is primarily to explain the *problem* that is the subject for the evening's study. Let's say it's the problem of the generation gap. The difficulty parents have in coping with their teenage children, the problem that older church members have in understanding the young people in the church.

2. Decide how the problem is to be illustrated

Most problems could be illustrated in many different ways. Of course it's possible for the study leader to have prepared the 'scenario', the drama, the situation to be acted out, ahead of time. That might be all right for the first time the group tackles role-play, but actually it's much better to allow the decision on the story to be acted out to be step two, taken by the group at the meeting.

So the group discusses possible stories. It could be a home scene with Jill just going out with her friend Anne to someone's birthday party and a decision on the time at which she should get home. It could be a scene at church after the evening service, maybe in the hall when people are having a cup of tea. Some older people are talking about the young people who turned up late: the young people in the tea queue respond with examples of older people who are always late, and with an explanation of why they couldn't help being late, and why lateness doesn't matter anyway.

3. Assign roles

It's much the best thing to allow people to volunteer for a particular role. A volunteer often has something that he really wants to say, and maybe has wanted to say for a long time. This is a marvellous opportunity to say it, but to say it *safely*.

Incidentally, note that some people are needed as observers, and their part in the evening's activity is extremely valuable.

4. Discussion by the participants

They may need just a few minutes, say five minutes, to 'warm up', to get the feel of their new characters, even to try a preliminary 'conversation' with one of the other characters. This 'chunk' must not be allowed to become a kind of 'dress rehearsal', as that removes the vital element of spontaneity.

5. The play itself

This should be directed towards a maximum of ten minutes, but in fact the study leader may want to stop it before that time once the principal point has been made.

6. Response

It is extremely important to allow the actors to comment on their feelings *immediately*, before the impact has begun to wear off, before they have time to begin to cover up, rationalize their behaviour. And then, when they have finished, the observers comment, both on the points that appeared to be made by the play itself, and on the effect that role-play had on the individuals involved.

7. Summary

Finally the study leader sums up.

Alternatively the group may decide to use fairly straightforward 'drama'. A simple presentation of the story of the 'rich fool' in Luke 12, for example. Or the group could try up-dating a parable. Get four or five of the house group to up-date the parable of the great banquet (Lk 14) so as to bring out the modern parallel. Or there's the parable in Luke 18 about the Pharisee and the tax collector. (What trades would Jesus choose if he were telling that story today?)

Of course, as any teacher knows, the great value of drama is that people get involved: they stop being merely passive observers. And, as we've seen already, modern educational thinking emphasizes the importance of involvement.

Study-a-book

Although this is often *said* to be the purpose of a house group meeting, in fact it usually turns out to be merely the study of some parts of a book. Only very rarely does a group end up by really understanding the whole book, a whole gospel, a complete letter.

A complete book should only be chosen for group study *as a book* if it has one of two characteristics: it must be short enough *or* it must be coherent enough.

By 'coherent' I mean simply that the ideas of the book hang together well. It's fairly clear why chapter six follows chapter five. The connection may be historical, as with the book of Genesis (this happened next), or it may be logical as in the letter to the church at Rome (if all that is true then this is what necessarily follows). Both Genesis and Romans are rather long books, but they are both easily outlined. Jeremiah is a long book which is almost impossible to outline, and 1 Peter is a short letter which contains a lot of self-contained paragraphs, dealing with many important subjects, but the subjects are not obviously related to one another.

Take the example of Romans. I have always been immensely grateful for the Keswick Convention Bible readings where Graham Scroggie took us through Romans. For the first time I had a firm grip on the total argument of a book of the Bible. This isn't his outline exactly, but it's very close to it:

1:1–17	INTRODUCTION	
1:18–3:20	CONDEMNATION	We have all gone wrong
3:21–5:21	SALVATION	How we may all be put right
6:1–8:39	SANCTIFICATION	How we can live right in the future
9:1–11:36	QUESTION	What about the Jews?
12:1–15:33	APPLICATION	This is how we should live as Christians
16:1–27	CONCLUSION	

A word of caution here: outlines aren't produced by committees or house groups. They are produced by individuals who have time to do it. Your house group won't produce an outline. The study leader produces it, explains it, and then the group uses it, and may even want to modify it a bit.

Other Bible books that *can* be studied as books would include Genesis, Exodus, Joshua, Judges, Ruth, Nehemiah, Esther, Daniel, John, 1 Corinthians, Galatians, Colossians, both of the letters to the Thessalonians, 2 Timothy, Hebrews and Revelation.

If you do plan on producing an outline, you simply must use a visual aid. I've already referred to the flip-pad. Practice writing with a felt-tipped pen beforehand so that you can at least write legibly and straight. Never attempt to put too much on one sheet: about a dozen or fifteen lines of writing, with only six or seven words to a line.

A flip-pad really is a most useful thing for a house group to own. It can be used not only for study outlines, but also for writing up prayer requests...and to avoid the need for giving out notices.

ROMANS
1:1-7 Introduction
1:8-3:20 Condemnation
3:20-5:21 Salvation
6:1-8:39 Sanctification
9:1-11:36 Question
12:1-15:33 Application
16:1-27 Conclusion

Some kind of stand for the flip-pad is useful. Not many people appreciate having drawing pins stuck into the wall or mantel to suspend the pad from!

An alternative to the flip-pad is the dry-marker board. This gives you a special white plastic surface on which to write with special felt-tipped pens. The writing is easily cleaned off with a dry cloth. This avoids the clouds of chalk dust that accompany a blackboard, and also avoids the search for a damp cloth to clean off writing from the ordinary kind of white board. Just one point about dry marker boards: writing should be cleaned off as soon as it's not needed. If it's left on the board for several days it becomes very difficult to remove.

Analysis

For this kind of study, too, you need the flip-pad. The aim is to take a chapter or even part of a long chapter, and break it up into its main parts.

Take Luke 12, for example. Modern translations like the NIV provide a helpful indication of the main divisions and it really doesn't make much sense to do that part of the work all over again. However, in this chapter, verses 13-34 seem to be especially related to each other. This part of the chapter could be analysed on the flip-pad during the house group meeting. Resist the temptation in this case to have it all neatly written up before the meeting. Actually watching the analysis being done is an important part of the learning process. Everybody can keep one eye on the passage itself while they have the other eye on the flip-pad, and so they can actually see how the whole process works. Hopefully they will be able to do the same sort of thing for themselves, later on, perhaps when they are preparing to lead a Bible study.

View-a-video

The resources of the house group don't end with the particular gifts of the members of the group, nor even with the various abilities of the other members of the church. There is a great deal of assistance available from organizations like Scripture Union, and video programmes are distributed by several Christian groups.

The particular point of a video is that videos use TVs, and the TV is primarily intended for the small group. G1 family groups and G2 small groups are just the right size for watching the little screen. Christian videos usually come with suggestions as to how to use them, often with discussion points for use in groups such as house groups. Incidentally there's no need to restrict your thinking to Christian videos. There are some excellent videos on topics like drug abuse put out by non-Christian organizations.

CHECK SHEET NUMBER TWO

Before you go any further, try answering these questions which all relate to chapters 4–6 of this book.

1. List the four leaders that a house group might need:
   - a) _____
   - b) _____
   - c) _____
   - d) _____

2. What are the four characteristics of an education programme?
   - a) _____
   - b) _____
   - c) _____
   - d) _____

3. Get together with at least two other people from your church and produce an outline for just one month of a CEP specially suited to your church at the present time.

4. A Bible study. Read the letter to Titus right through at least five times.
   a. On a large piece of paper write down the five groups that are said to need special teaching. In a second column write down *what* each group was to be taught. In a third column write down who was to do the teaching in each case.
   b. Another five: write down five characteristics that Titus was to show in his teaching. Titus 2:15 talks about *authority*. How can we teach with *authority* today?
   c. Go through Titus again, verse by verse, with the CEP chart, page 62, in front of you. Tick off each item in that chart that is also mentioned in Titus. You'll need to work carefully, matching what Paul says to Titus to what I've put in the chart.
      Which items in the chart do *not* appear in Titus? Can you think of an explanation for some being missing?

CHAPTER 7

House Groups and Evangelism

The house group *can* be used for evangelism. But that does *not* mean bringing in an evangelist and singing 'Just as I am'. In fact quite the contrary: it may mean that you don't do any singing at all.

But house groups can be a very powerful means of reaching out to people who aren't committed Christians, mainly just because they *are* house groups, groups of Christians who meet in houses rather than in special 'church' buildings. Church buildings really can act as an effective deterrent to people who would actually quite like to find out about Christianity. Such people often don't know what goes on inside the doors of a church and that rather unnerves them. Anglicans have a slight advantage here, because people still go to anglican churches for weddings and christenings. But as to what goes on in a baptist church or a methodist church...they have as much idea of that as they have about what goes on in the Kremlin on a Friday night. In other words they haven't a clue. And men in particular are very hesitant about going into strange places.

Another reason why house groups are so good for outreach is because churches are so bad. So-called evangelistic services in the churches seem to be devoted to activities guaranteed to exclude people who aren't Christians. They usually start with a hymn and a prayer...both of them activities which are very suitable for Christians, but rather odd to impose on, say, a Muslim. The result is that the church, through its evangelistic services, tends to reach people who are already on the fringe of the church, but leaves outside the masses of the totally unchurched. Well...for them there is the house group.

An outreach evening

Let's try to ensure that we don't make the same mistakes here as have been made in evangelistic services in the churches. Instead of pushing ahead with planning the outreach evening, let's start by thinking about the people we're trying to get in. What do they want? How do they feel?

First of all they probably can't actually put into words what they want. But the number one problem that most people have today is that life doesn't seem to make sense. If you're old, life doesn't seem to make sense because having spent a lifetime acquiring a bit of understanding, a bit of knowledge, life's end suddenly becomes a reality and, what's perhaps worse, the intellect begins to sag. If you're young, life doesn't seem to make sense because either there's little chance of getting a job, or the job you can get isn't really what you want. And in between there are all the problems of a world wasting its resources on nuclear weapons and fleets of bombers, and moon-shots and satellites, while every day thousands starve to death. I think that what people *want* is for life to make sense. For someone to come along and explain this apparently crazy world.

How do they feel? They probably feel nervous about going to any sort of 'meeting'. Nowadays even trade union meetings attract only the dedicated. Other types of meetings are dead ducks today.

Negatively we can talk about what the people out there

don't want. What they don't want is an invitation to go to church. What they don't want is a snap answer, a glib response ('the real problem, brother, is *sin*'). What they don't want is a handful of proof texts. And what they don't want is an invitation to sit in someone's house with a bunch of people they've never met before, trying to make polite conversation.

Now to meet their needs, demands more than a neatly printed card inviting these folks to a friendly house-group meeting. There's a lot of work to be done long before that stage can be reached. Christians who want the privilege of helping their neighbours spiritually must be prepared to spend time showing that they care for the neighbours practically. We need to get to know people. *Really* know them. Washing the cars together, borrowing his lawn-mower, maybe going to a soccer match together, or a trip to the Sales together. All sorts of things that will enable us to know our neighbours as people, and to allow them to see us as people.

And, of course, it's the wise Christian who is prepared to let his neighbours do *him* a favour. It's a drag to be always on the receiving end of charity: 'You'll recognize Eddie because he'll be doing someone an act of kindness. And you'll recognize the someone by the harassed expression on his face!' It really is important that our approach to our neighbours should be the expression of a real, genuine interest in them. They must never be seen as mere scalps to be hung on our evangelical belts.

Well now, let's suppose that you really do know your neighbours, and they have come to know you, and they have perhaps shown some kind of interest in your faith. And let's suppose that the house group has set aside an evening when such friends will be made welcome and their needs particularly catered for. How is the evening to be used?

Well, obviously you'll need to have a reasonable idea of just how many visitors are seriously expected. So that there will be tea and coffee to go round. And so that some of the house group regulars can be asked to stay away if necessary. Not because they are a potential embarrassment, but because it is important to get the balance between Christian regulars and uncommitted visitors right. Not so *few* Christians that it looks as though you're quite desperate for new blood, but not so *many* Christians that the visitors feel as though they are being got at.

There are four fundamentals to have in mind as you plan the evening, so we'll have a look at each of these.

1. To get your visitors in and feeling at home

There ought not to be too much difficulty here. Firstly, they are coming into a home that's probably quite similar to their own, so they don't feel out of place. Secondly, because you have got to know them quite well over the past few months they know you'll keep an eye on them. They trust you as friends. And of course you'll be sure to introduce them to just a few of the other folks: the people whose home it is and the study leader for the evening, at least. Obviously, trying to introduce them to *everybody* would be a sheer waste of time.

If you really want your visitors to feel at home, you don't want to have the Christians sitting around with solemn expressions on their faces and big leather Bibles under their arms....

Background music isn't at all a bad thing, but be sure it's appropriate. I must confess here to a major no-no that I have: I wince every time I hear 'Jesu joy of man's desiring' or 'Sheep may safely graze' used as a sort of epitome of Christian music. The music bit really needs someone who has some knowledge of music and can produce music with a little originality about it. There really are some magnificent songs around which could lead in to useful conversations, even in the comparative racket of a house group.

2. Make sure that they learn something

This requires that you sit down long before the meeting to decide what you feel it might be appropriate for them to learn. Keep the aim modest. Too many speakers feel bullied into trying to put over the whole Christian package every time they speak. The incarnation and the crucifixion and the resurrection and the ascension and Pentecost and judgement and heaven and hell and Daniel's seventieth week too if they can manage to fit it in.

There's a kind of blackmailing attitude there among the professional critics of the preachers. I know perfectly well that at the bigger churches and conventions there are people out there who don't want to hear what God might have to say through Peter Cotterell. They want to know if Peter Cotterell is 'sound'. And woe betide Peter Cotterell if he leaves out any of the formidable list of subjects which together add up to a sound address. Ordinary Christians can have little idea of the stream of bits of paper handed to and sent to speakers by earnest, vocal critics in the congregations. Wisdom, it would seem, will die out with them. But this kind of pressure really must be resisted. Ask God to show you through his Spirit what he wants taught, and be content to teach that. Even if there are people around who want more and more added in. Do it God's way.

So it's a question of being satisfied that the visitors learn something, and not expecting that they'll learn everything at once. It might be enough for them to learn that all religions are *not* the same, or that the world's problems really have their starting point in human greed, or that the resurrection of Jesus *is* important and not an optional extra, or that it *is* a good thing to go to church, or that a good life does *not* depend on acquiring *things*. (Luke 12:15 is a fine starting point here: if a man's life does not consist in the abundance of his possessions, what does it consist in?)

It is important that you have a clear idea of just what your visitors should learn during the evening. To be quite sure that you know what it is write it down in a single sentence. And then ask afterwards: did they learn that?

3. Give them adequate opportunity to ask their questions.

There are two ways of setting about this: one is simply to timetable a spot in the programme where you ask, 'Now, does anyone have any questions?' Stone cold. Just like that. Almost certainly you won't get any. Afterwards you may comfort yourself with the thought that you gave them an opportunity to ask questions, and blame the dullness of the visitors for the zero response. But is that approach really going to give them an *adequate* opportunity for asking questions? Is that the way questions normally appear? Surely questions are positively *provoked*. And this is the other way of setting about the task of giving the visitors an adequate opportunity to ask their questions: by *provoking* questions. And you will provoke questions when what you say is actually relevant to your visitors. Understandable but provocative. By provocative I mean that you say things which cut across normal ideas. As Jesus did. That example in Luke 12:15 is a marvellous example. You could talk about 'what makes life worthwhile' all evening. Especially if you resist the temptation to provide the answers all neatly pre-packaged. Provoke them to ask: 'Well, what *does* make life worthwhile, then?' Be prepared to prod them to suggest answers. Can they think of high spots in their lives? Can you? And more questions come: what made that a high spot?

My life's high spots are probably as odd as yours are. I recall one. I'd been camping, back in 1969, near Arundel with fifty or sixty lads. We had been canoeing, trekking, learning archery and playing soccer on the sands near Littlehampton. I was camp padre so I'd had a certain amount of talking to do. Early on in the two week camp my twin brother had joined us: 'the carbon copy' he was instantly dubbed. It was a great time, but very hard work. Then came the end of camp and all the bustle of striking tents and clearing the camp site. Finally they were all gone, and Cliff and I thought about supper. We went in to Littlehampton as the sun was setting. It had been a beautiful day. We found a little cafe, looking over the river Arun, and ordered fish and chips. All very ordinary. But *as I sat there* I knew this was going to be one of my great memories.

Now then: what does man's life consist of?

Before we leave this matter of answering questions, a word of warning. Be ready to admit: 'I don't know the answer to that question.' No one minds the confession that you don't know everything, that you don't have all the answers. What people do mind is bluff, a smoke-screen of words, what is expressively labelled 'guff'. If you don't know the answer, say that you don't know, but then move to an assurance that you'll find out for next time. That just might be enough to bring 'em back!

4. Send the visitors away at the end both satisfied and dissatisfied.

They should go away with this contradictory mixture of feelings: 'That was interesting. Not at all what I'd expected. Glad I went. I'd never have thought of that. They seemed a nice bunch of people. Time really flew tonight. I didn't think that Christianity was like that at all...I wonder how they can be so sure. I still don't quite understand this praying business, but it seemed quite natural to them. I still don't see why Nicodemus wasn't good enough for God—he seemed to be a very religious sort of person. I wish my life made sense...don't really know what it's all about....'

With *that* mixture of responses he's likely to be back.

Non-stop house group outreach

Visitors should *always* be welcome at any church house group. It's not necessary to wait for some special 'outreach evening' before people can invite friends who are not yet committed Christians. Many house groups work positively at getting friends and neighbours in every week. Of course that can slow things up in the house group, as the visitors may know very little and ask a lot of rather basic questions and raise all sorts of objections.

If this continual questioning becomes a problem, it might be a good idea to suggest starting a new house group especially for those who have questions!

And then there's the question: where is the new group to meet? This brings us to another very powerful possibility: don't have the house group in the home of a church member, but in the home of one of those who has questions.

This really is a marvellous way to reach out to interested neighbours. Or you can take the idea even further. Some churches arrange a programme where Christians visit the houses in the area, looking for people who have questions, and inviting them to set up house groups which the church will then staff, so far as *teaching* is concerned. The offer is usually made, for, say, six weeks. Then if asked, they can offer another period of six weeks, although it is wise to allow a break in between, so that you clearly are giving *two* six-week sessions, which most families can cope with, and not twelve weeks of study, which can seem interminable.

This approach throws a lot of the responsibility back on those who are interested, and it means that they can have teaching, and can ask their questions in a setting where they are *literally* at home. So you allow them to arrange the refreshments and invite the neighbours, while you come in as a minority of two (the small team approach is *much* better than leaving it to one individual), ready to teach, listen and answer questions.

What to teach? In the first period let *them* set the agenda. If you have an invitation for a second spell, offer them a carefully thought out programme of talks and discussions (note 2 Tim 4:3).

CHAPTER 8

When There Is A Fight

As we have seen, the house group is a mixture of three types of small group. It is a *friendship* group, it is a *work* group and it is a *care* group. Conflict from within the group can appear as a result of the fact that the house group is a kind of hybrid small group.

For example, if we think of a more typical work group, a group of mechanics in a garage, we'll see that they didn't get their jobs because they were already pals and they didn't get their jobs so that they could become pals. They got their jobs because there was work to be done and they were trained to do it.

True enough the work in the garage couldn't really go on if the men were always arguing, or, worse still, if they wouldn't even speak to each other. So a certain level of friendship is essential even in a genuine work group. On the other hand, disagreement isn't forbidden. If George discovers a better way of fitting a new exhaust system, he doesn't have to keep the idea to himself just because no one else has ever thought of doing the job that way. Nor does he have to worry too much even if Ernie is the one who set up the way the job is done now. He'll probably try the new method out himself a few times, then talk it over with the foreman, and maybe they will decide to change the current working practice for changing exhausts. Disagreement can be very productive.

Now let's transfer this kind of thinking to the house group. The house group *is* a friendship group (as well as a work group) and there is a tendency, often encouraged by the minister and other leaders, to conform. We all say the same thing about everything, even if, inside, we're not at all sure that we *do* agree. Still, we don't want to upset the apple-cart. Don't want to start an argument. Don't want to get Ernie upset. But that's really very unrealistic. Of *course* we disagree about some things. Sometimes we do understand the subject and genuinely disagree with the conclusions of other people. Sometimes we disagree simply because we don't understand. But disagreement is part of life. There are probably no two Christians anywhere who agree with one another about everything.

Now it's through talking about these honestly held differences that a group grows. Growth not merely in soundly based knowledge, but growth also in graciousness: recognizing that we are *allowed* to have genuine differences of opinion, and that people who disagree with us are not necessarily pig-headed heretics or incurably dumb. Maturity does not come merely through holding on to a collection of beliefs without ever listening (carefully, respectfully, prayerfully) to people who think differently.

Always we have to keep in mind A.W. Tozer's phrase: 'Some things are not negotiable.' But it is too easy for Christians to become tight-lipped, unloving, self-righteous people who will never listen to others, never submit their systems to any kind of critical scrutiny. Those who disagree with them *must* be 'liberals', 'modernists', even 'heretics'. These are labels often used unfairly and unkindly of folks whose principal fault is that they disagree with us.

Why people disagree

If a disagreement is to be settled properly, used constructively, instead of merely being swept under the carpet, it is important to know the *real* reason for the disagreement. We all know that when Mrs Thomas disagrees with Mr Thomas about when they should have their holiday this year, the argument probably has little to do with the question of the weather in the first week of August against the weather in the third week. It might have a lot to do with the fact that Mr T spent more than two hundred pounds on a computer without asking his wife's opinion at all.

Now that kind of problem spills over into the house group. So when Mr T agrees that the 'thousand years' mentioned in Revelation 20 means just what it says, a real, thousand years, and Mrs T stridently disagrees and suggests that the number one thousand is just symbolic, the argument may have nothing to do with the Bible. It may have a lot to do with plans for the summer holiday, or pocket money for the children, or a new pair of shoes. Or that computer.

Obviously that produces a problem for the house group: in fact two problems. Firstly, you can't discuss the thousand years business sensibly. Mr and Mrs T aren't arguing sensibly. They're not really arguing about the 'millenium' at all. So the argument, and that's what it is, an argument, becomes absurd and there is far more heat in it than there is light. The second problem, obviously, is that settling the argument about the thousand years doesn't really settle the argument at all. That argument, the real argument, will break out again as soon as you reach Gog and Magog further on in the same chapter.

So, perhaps from an unexpected direction, we come upon an important principle to be observed when trying to settle arguments, when trying to answer questions: find out what the *real* point of disagreement is, find out what the real question is. That principle applies far beyond mere questions being asked by Mr and Mrs T. I've been made to feel very foolish time and time again because I've been cheerfully and authoritatively answering a question which hasn't been asked!

Now let's see if we can identify the principal causes of disagreements. We've already found one: disagreements between members of a family, actually reflecting some profound family problem.

Secondly, there are disagreements which arise from *racial prejudice*. This goes all the way from despising the cockney accent, through disliking Americans, to the colour thing and being unable to get along with blacks. I would even include in this category the problem of men who can't get along with women and women who despise men. I think that it includes middle class people who look down on less well educated neighbours, and the less educated people who turn off to anyone who 'speaks posh'.

Thirdly, there's theological prejudice. You do find people in house groups who already know all the answers because they have a complete theological package, gift-wrapped and available to anyone who will take on the whole thing. They have no intention of unwrapping it to see how it works, nor of rearranging the contents, not for anyone's sake. Not even for the sake of the Bible.

Fourthly, there are arguments, a bit like the arguments that occur within the family, that are really the left-overs of arguments between the same people on some previous occasion.

Fifthly, there are arguments that begin just because someone in the group is naturally argumentative. He can always find an alternative way of looking at any subject at all, and can always find an alternative answer to any question.

Sixthly, there are arguments that develop, as we sometimes say, because someone in the group wants to show off. More accurately, someone is drawing attention to his own prior claim to group leadership. *He* has the answers; why doesn't the group ask *him*?

And finally the seventh reason for arguments, the arguments that *ought* to take place simply because there is an honest disagreement about the answer to the question, and the right answer is by no means obvious.

No matter how a disagreement may arise it is important for the health of the house group to settle the disagreement. Continual disagreement and fruitless argument wears away group cohesion. The group begins to come apart. It's worth just briefly suggesting why this is so.

Within any genuine *group* (a crowd is not really a group at all) the key to group relationships is found in the relationship between *pairs* of people, *dyads* as they are called. Ultimately all group behaviour can be seen to be dyadic. One person doesn't have a relationship to the whole group: he has a relationship with one other person in the group and that determines how he relates to everyone else. So if Mr and Mrs T are having a running battle about that computer, their dyad will affect the rest of the group. Individuals may become impatient with both of them, or may take sides, but the group confusion really goes back to the squabble between Mr and Mrs T, back to their dyad. You can see it for yourself at almost any house-group meeting. If one dyad has a particularly strong relationship that evening, *really* good or *really* bad, then that relationship is likely to determine the house group's balance that evening.

I was minister of an International Church in Addis Ababa for about ten years. For part of that time I had a superb pianist to lead the singing. By superb, I don't merely mean that she was just a good pianist. She was superb for a different reason: she was a no-problem person. She didn't take offence if I wanted something sung a bit faster. She wasn't upset if, at the last minute, I decided to change the final hymn. She didn't even mind if we didn't *have* a final hymn. I think the dyad between the pianist and me was a major influence on the church.

If you don't agree, think of the situation in some churches where, if the preacher does try to change anything in the musical arrangements, there is a muffled but

entirely audible explosion from the direction of the organ:
'Well, I wish you'd warned me...how do you expect me
to find the right tune at this time of night...how would
you like it if....' The same sort of dyadic situation can
apply to the minister and the song leader (if you are
fortunate enough to be allowed to have one) or the
minister and the church secretary, or the vicar and the
choir master. Dyads make or break group relationships.

So, then, if you have an entrenched battling dyad in
your house group it's a bit like having a grumbling appendix. An operation may become necessary at any time, for
the sake of the health of the whole body.

I say that arguments and disagreements, should not just
be allowed to go on, but there should be an attempt made
to settle them. There's a good example in Paul's letter to
the church at Philippi. Paul wrote to the whole church,
and included a plea to Euodia and Syntyche (a dyad) to
settle their disagreement. I wonder how those two ladies
felt when that letter was read out on Sunday? Sunset in
glorious technicolour, I suspect. But Paul didn't include
that appeal just to embarrass them. My guess is that the
church was really being upset by that one dyad (Phil 4:2).

Types of disagreement

1. Disagreements that arise because of a family feud

Two things to note here. Firstly, that most churches don't
offer any help until the breakdown point is reached. That's
much too late. Secondly, because most Christian families
know that divorce or even formal separation, is simply not
on, breakdown point is never reached. The appendix is
allowed to go on grumbling, year in, year out. And so the
husband *always* contradicts his wife, the wife *always* has
some complaint to make about her husband. Their dyadic
relationship is painfully clear in the house group and
ought to be tackled by the house group in its caring role.

But how should the problem be tackled? In the house-group meeting you simply deal with the immediate disagreement. Tactfully and honestly, but so far as possible ignoring the personality clash. But still a way must be found to deal with the real problem. The right person has to be found to deal with it, and that's probably not the minister. The tradition in the church is probably that *he* is only called in when there's serious trouble. And tongues might wag if the minister is called in before the serious trouble has really appeared. No, not the minister. Better someone from the house group. Not necessarily someone with a Diploma in Psychology, but someone who will be able to initially get the confidence of at least *one* of them, and eventually both. Even stating the problem can be of help to a couple who are in the early stages of deep disagreement. Once a neutral outsider has stated the problem it is usually easier for the couple to discuss it. And after that they may need to take the initiative of approaching someone else who could give them sensible advice.

But don't forget: the constant nagging pain of a husband/wife dyad in conflict can seriously damage your house group.

2. *Disagreements that arise because of people prejudice*

Every Christian should at some time get involved in a long and serious discussion about this problem, a discussion led by someone who is qualified to talk about it. The fact is that we are all prejudiced. Against Americans, the Irish, against Pakistanis, against whites, against the rich, against the poor, against gypsies, against ministers.... The list of possible people prejudices is endless.

Few of us know what our people prejudices are. Some of us even pretend that we don't have any people prejudice at all. I remember talking with a group of young people about this, and they were really upset by my insistence that we are all prejudiced. They flatly denied it. That problem was a problem for my generation, but not theirs. Now it so happened that two of these young people were to be married shortly. They hadn't yet managed to find a place to live. Houses in their own area were so expensive. The church was not too far from Southall, a town with a very large immigrant population. House prices there, I knew, were very reasonable. So I suggested that the couple might buy a house there in Southall. Without stopping to think the girl burst out: 'Oh, I couldn't live there, with all those....' but she didn't finish her sentence. She blushed bright red...and everyone got the point. Southall, where a white face is something of an exception, where you can buy a real *sari*, eat a real curry, overhear most of the languages of Asia. She didn't want to live *there*! And now she knew that she was prejudiced.

I have little patience with people who tell me that they aren't prejudiced. What I want to know is: do you know what your prejudices are, and what are you doing about them?

So how is prejudice dealt with in the house group? Well, I've already indicated that every Christian should share in a thorough discussion of the whole subject. So that could be arranged as one of the house-group activities.

Secondly, it is very effective if the study leader has already identified some of the prejudices of the group. We give ourselves away in our normal conversation, with jokes about other races, for example. So actually to draw attention to some of the prejudices that have been observed, say in the past six months, could bring people up with a jerk. Wow! Are we really like that?

Thirdly, admit to the prejudice. Don't try to find an alibi, an explanation. Just admit to it. At the house-group meeting invite people to write down the sort of people they are prejudiced against. Do *not* invite them to read out their lists. That can do a lot of harm.

But fourthly have the whole group spend time in praying about their prejudices: quiet, silent, individual prayer for deliverance from prejudice that has been identified. Open prayer asking for God's help in being ready to admit to this sin, and for a willingness to look to God for his help in dealing with it.

And fifthly, if you are aware of a particular people prejudice, try to get to know a family from that particular people. Over a cup of tea miracles of healing have been experienced as God's people have realized their God-given privilege of being 'all one in Christ Jesus'.

3. Disagreements that arise out of theological prejudice

Theological prejudice is usually the problem of the amateur theologian. Although the person who has studied theology is still likely to have many prejudices, at least he will be likely to know some of them, and to admit that more than one view is entirely possible. And usually he knows how little he knows. I have to admit that when I was twenty, four years on as a Christian, I had theology all worked out. Daniel and Revelation were neatly dia-grammed, their mysteries all unravelled. What was that marvellous example cited by Donald Barnhouse years back at Keswick: he held up a booklet, little more than a tract, 'The Holy Spirit explained', price two pence!! That was about my level. I really *cringe* now as I think back to those days. I honestly don't think that a lot of study has made me big headed: I think that I'm less dogmatic now, more open to correction. Except...I must confess that I am very dogmatic about people who are very dogmatic....

Let me say that I don't believe that we can produce a complete 'systematic theology', a system which answers all the theological questions, taking in all the evidence, leaving no holes. God is too great for us to be able to box him into any system of our making. Systematic theology soon falls into the trap of telling God what he can do and what he can't do and what he must do. And it's just then that he turns around and does what he *wills* to do.

I was in a Brethren church once, and they asked me to

talk to their young people about churches that grow. I told them about a church I knew, in London, with a congregation made up equally of blacks and whites. It was a striking example of a happy church, a united church, and it was a growing church. In the discussion afterwards, one of the young men insisted: 'But it *can't* be growing because it isn't homogeneous, and that's one of the seven Vital Signs [you could hear the capital letters as he spoke] for growth.' He had read in a book that churches will only grow if they demonstrate these seven 'Vital Signs', one of which was homogeneity: the church must consist of people of just one sort. Here was a mixed congregation, so it *couldn't* grow. God, the Holy Spirit, wasn't allowed to save people there! But because God is God he went right ahead and did what he wanted to do.

That's just one example. But people lay down all sorts of conditions—for salvation, for example. First you must repent. Then you must believe in God, actually in the Trinity. You must believe in the Bible. You must believe in the 'substitutionary atonement'. The modern 'must' concerns the Holy Spirit: the Spirit-filled Christian *must* speak in tongues. We create all kinds of rules, rules to manipulate God. And the book of rules may easily come between a Christian and his Bible. He may find it impossible to 'see' some verses in the Bible because his rule book either doesn't allow for them or actually runs contrary to them.

It really is important for every Christian to know, and to accept the fact, that there are dozens of systematic theologies, all different, all held sincerely by fine Christian people. And it's a brave man who insists that his system and no other is the right one.

I've often said that producing a systematic theology is a bit like trying to make a spaghetti sandwich. As fast as you push the spaghetti into one end of the sandwich, so bits fall out of the other end of it. As fast as you cram texts into one end of your systematic theology, so other texts drop out of the other end. They won't all fit. And then someone else comes along and excavates all those texts that your system left out and produces a different systematic theology, but in turn leaving out some of the bits that you managed to fit in.

In the 'modern' sense Jesus himself was unsystematic. Take the Sermon on the Mount, for example. In Matthew 5:16 Jesus tells us that we are to let our light shine before men so that 'they may see your good deeds and praise your Father in heaven'. Read on, and in Matthew 6:1 Jesus says: 'Be careful not to do your "acts of righteousness" before men, to be seen by them.'

You see, Jesus is not producing a systematic theology, a neat set of rules. He is considering the individual and his motives, not mankind as a whole. To produce a set of rules that would cover every possible situation would make the rules too complex—impossible for ordinary people to understand. As the Pharisees and the Scribes had found out.

According to the rules they had worked out, on the Sabbath a Jewish mother could push her child along, or pull her child along, but couldn't *drag* her child along. If the child managed to dislocate a bone as they struggled, the mother couldn't deliberately treat the dislocation with cold water, but she was allowed to wash the limb in the usual way—and if she managed, as it were accidentally, to slip the bone back into place again, well, rather grudgingly the law admitted: the child was healed.

Meanwhile her husband could lead their camels out using the usual lead ropes, but had to take care not to allow the individual ropes to twine together in his hand because that would be work. And if he dropped a barrel of wine he could mop up enough wine for three meals, just so long as he didn't use a sponge for the task that had to be squeezed out. And if he was unfortunate and couldn't rescue any of the wine then he could borrow some from his neighbour provided that he didn't actually *ask* to borrow it. And with his glass of wine in front of him he could sit down to write just one letter, but couldn't make a copy of it. Not on the Sabbath. Now that's how the Pharisees and the Scribes worked: trying to produce the complete system. But human life was simply too varied for them: the system continually broke down. And so do our systematic theologies.

So let us all understand, humbly, that our authority is the Bible, with all its diversity and richness, not some human system extracted from it.

4. Disagreements that arise out of people quarrels

These are very similar in nature to quarrels between husband and wife. The particular difficulty here, however, is to discover just why *these* two people disagree with one another so regularly. What is the special relationship which so obviously links them? To discover the answer you may need to know the history of the church, possibly going back a good many years.

As is so often the case, in people quarrels, the original cause of the disagreement may turn out to have been quite trivial. Obviously that's by no means always the case, but it often is. Unfortunately, misunderstandings that are allowed to remain unresolved do not usually fade into insignificance but grow, almost in proportion to the rate at which the memory of the original fight fades. The Bible pattern is not to allow misunderstandings to remain unresolved overnight (Eph 4:26).

For everyone's sake these long-standing disagreements need to be sorted out. It is likely that a good many other church activities have been in some measure soured by them before they arise in the house group, so it really is important to find some spiritually-minded Christian to help the dyad sort out its problems. It must be admitted, though, that these are particularly difficult problems to work through. They often occur between spiritual leaders who may refuse to recognize even that there *is* a problem.

I recall only too well just such a situation between two men who had been at odds with each other for more than a decade. And in a gathering of the leaders of that church one of the men insisted: 'There's nothing between George and me. Nothing at all, is there, George?' And George cheerfully confirmed what everybody else knew to be nonsense, that there was nothing between them.

Certainly such disagreements, with roots reaching way back into the past, won't be easily resolved, and if the people concerned refuse to recognize the problem they *can't* be resolved. In such cases one can only leave the matter and pray that a more open spirit may come. But it is important that someone should make clear to those involved in the disagreement that there is a problem. Even if they do deny it. Then the Holy Spirit is set free to do his work of convicting them.

5. Disagreements that start with people who are naturally argumentative

Actually, the person who appears to be naturally argumentative may well have a most valuable gift. Not the argumentative bit, but what lies behind the argumentative

Disagreements in the House Group

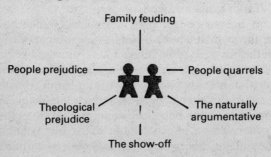

Family feuding

People prejudice — People quarrels

Theological prejudice — The naturally argumentative

The show-off

bit. The argumentative person is often the kind of person who can see another side to every question. Now that, surely, is better than the dogmatic person who can't see any alternative view at all?

The argumentative person may be upset by what he thinks is an unfair and prejudiced view. He wants to restore the balance. On the front page of the newspaper recently was a paragraph about a member of the Royal Family who had been involved in a car crash. The paragraph went on to say that he had been breathalysed. That was on the front page. Inside there was more about it. But *inside* it said that the breath test was negative. He hadn't been drinking. Now with just the front page summary, my guess is that most people would at once have assumed that he had been drinking, 'Otherwise why would they put that in, about a breath test?' Well, I could think of another reason: to sell newspapers. So I might have got into an argument over that story, or over an account of a church member seen going into a pub or walking around London's Soho or even being seen with a woman who was not his wife. (Incidentally my twin brother, and we *are* identical, takes delight in walking round the shops near the church where I worship, hand in hand with his wife. And responding cheerfully to people who greet him with a 'Hi, Peter!' *Honi soit qui mal y pense* as the man said.)

Still, it has to be admitted that the argumentative person, the person who can always see another way of interpreting facts, may be rather trying. Because he can always see several possibilities it is very difficult to find out just what he believes about anything. However, the *mature* use of this gift can be of immense value to a group, enabling everyone to be a little more cautious than they might otherwise be. A little more charitable, possibly, than they might otherwise be. A little more charitable, possibly, than they would be without him.

As we have already seen, some things are not negotiable. The naturally argumentative person is in real danger of having no firm foundation for his faith. There are subjects where a certain amount of dogmatism is desirable. Tolerance may be misplaced:

> Sometimes with secret pride I sigh,
> and think, 'How tolerant am I!'
> Then pause, and wonder, 'Which is mine,
> tolerance—or a rubber spine?'

The naturally argumentative person may need help to see himself as others see him, and to enable him to use his gift with discernment.

6. Disagreements that arise because of someone trying to draw attention to himself

These disagreements are difficult to handle, because often the person concerned is trying to show off how much he knows, and by contrast how little the study leader knows, and, perhaps, to suggest that *he* should be the study leader. If you are the leader you could be reacting to him in quite the wrong way and for quite the wrong reason.

Still, pride *is* a very serious sin, and this kind of person has a rather unhealthy dose of it and should be helped. But pride is a *crude* sort of sin, not at all subtle, so that the sin is usually obvious to everyone except the one who has it. Being a crude sort of sin it does not need any finesse in dealing with it. A blunt instrument is called for, not a feather duster.

I was once a student at Spurgeon's Theological College where much of the discipline was in the hands of the students. They had a sovereign remedy for incipient pride. They'd warn the offender, very gently, and if that didn't produce results the inevitable consequence was a cold bath. The victim was dumped into it by six or seven stalwarts. They didn't bother to take his clothes off. The cure seemed to work like a dream. I never knew of a case where the dose had to be repeated.

No, I know that we can't go around doing that kind of

thing in civilized society. But something as blunt as that may be called for. A metaphorical cold bath if not the real thing.

The seventh category of disagreement I don't need to deal with here, because it is legitimate argument, healthy disagreement.

Group stability

What happens to a house group when there is a disagreement? Obviously any disagreement tends to rock the boat. That's why a group that is *only* a friendship group discourages disagreements. But a work group, if it is to mature, become more effective, must allow the disagreements that are inevitably there to come out and be discussed.

So let's consider a house group that has been running for several weeks which is first and foremost a friendship group. All is going well. There have been no real disagreements so far. Group consensus is very high. That simply means that everyone in the house group seems to be agreed about almost everything.

Obviously they *aren't* agreed on pretty well everything. They are agreed merely on the handful of subjects they've talked about so far. Even then, several members of the group have probably kept their views to themselves. But now comes open disagreement.

Joe thinks that denominations are all wrong: we should get out of the whole system *now*. He points to John 17, and Jesus' prayer for unity. Jim doesn't agree. He can remember a time when the church was struggling and they were all only too pleased to get help 'from the denomination'. 'We wouldn't have this church now if it hadn't been for them up in London.'

Joe and Jim feel equally strongly about the matter. And they both speak with considerable warmth. So how does the house group respond? Firstly with dismay. Then with uncertainty: 'Now what do we do?' Group consensus drops as people take sides. The argument spreads, there is a certain amount of battle being done. Conflict.

The outcome of all this will depend on the way in which the disagreement is handled. There are two possible ways: try to banish it, to consign the disagreement to oblivion. Trust in time the great healer: 'By next week they'll have forgotten all about it.' Allow the dust to settle. But that might not be the best way. The wise leader may want to show the wisdom there is in both sides of the disagreement, to take a view that does justice to what both men are saying. Not ducking the real issues, but admitting the good, sound, Christian logic of each, and producing a balanced attitude to the question of denominations. A view that, hopefully, is also the view of the leadership of the church. In turn the church's leaders may need to be told of the discussion, and of the nature of the 'balanced view' so that the vicar won't cut right across it in next Sunday's sermon!

Now what happens in the house group? There is a *resolution* of the disagreement, and a new level of group consensus. If the disagreement has been well handled the group consensus will actually be higher than it was before. A new area of agreement has been added. By contrast, if the disagreement is wrongly handled the house group might be split, and the division could well become repeatedly apparent in future disagreements. In that case the new consensus is *lower* than the old and the house group has failed to profit from the disagreement.

GROUP STABILITY

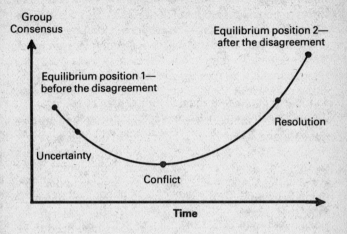

CHAPTER 9

Some Biblical Examples

The New Testament includes a number of examples of disagreements among Christians, and there's helpful advice about how such arguments ought to be dealt with.

Paul and Peter

A deep disagreement occurred at Antioch between Paul and Peter. Paul himself had been brought to Antioch by Barnabas (Acts 11:25–26), and he set to work teaching the new Christians. Now very early on the Christians were faced with a major question: what was the relationship between Judaism and Christianity? Were Christians a 'sect' of Judaism? Along with this question went another, very practical, question: were Christians to obey all the laws that the Scribes and Pharisees had put together—especially the rules about food?

To put it simply, Paul believed that they didn't and Peter believed that they did. At least...Peter wasn't too sure. I think that it was Peter's old weakness, really, that produced the trouble. Peter tended to be influenced by the crowd he was with. Remember, with the disciples he had been loud in his assurances that he would never betray Jesus (Mk 14:27–31), but with the crowd in the courtyard of the High Priest's house we find him cursing and swearing, disowning Jesus (Mk 14:66–72).

So when Peter paid a visit to Antioch and found a mixed church, Christians who had formerly been Jews, and Christians who had come out from other religions, all sitting together and eating together, he happily joined in.

Then came trouble. More visitors arrived...from Jerusalem. From the apostle, James. These newcomers most certainly did *not* approve of this mixture in the Antioch church. Of *course* Christians must observe the food laws of the Old Testament. *They* were not going to sit down to dinner with people who were eating food banned by the Law. And obviously Peter was afraid of them.

Perhaps he was afraid of the report they might take back to Jerusalem. So he made some kind of fumbling excuse and went off to have dinner somewhere else. It was hypocrisy.

At least that's what Paul called it in his account of the incident (Gal 2:1–21). Paul felt that he must take action. So he waited until Peter came back and had the whole matter out in the open. Not just Paul and Peter together, but in front of all the Christians.

I still have a little difficulty about that. My problem, of course, lies in Matthew 18. There, in verses 15–17, Jesus explained how his followers *ought* to settle their disagreements. Step one: go and talk personally to whomever it is you have the disagreement with. Try to sort things out just between the two of you. If he won't listen, then go back with one or two others, and see if together you can resolve matters. If he still won't listen, then, step three, is to tell the whole church. And then, if he won't pay attention to the church, stop worrying about the matter. You've done what you can to resolve the disagreement. Leave him alone.

Paul seems to have gone straight to step three, without even trying steps one and two. Mind you, he might have tried steps one and two without mentioning the fact. But thinking the matter through carefully, it seems that Jesus was talking about a very different kind of situation from the one Paul faced. Jesus was talking about two Christians, one of whom had done something against the other. Peter's error was not personal...it was an error directed

not against Paul but against the whole church at Antioch.
And so Paul settled the problem the way he did: before
the whole church.

So from Galatians 2 and Matthew 18 we obtain two
principles for dealing with disagreements. From Matthew
we learn that personal disagreements should be dealt with
personally, if at all possible. From Galatians we learn that
where doctrine is concerned it's best to have a disagreement in the open, before the whole church, even if
some people get upset, than to allow wrong teaching to go
uncorrected.

Euodia and Syntyche

We've already met this couple whose disagreement is
mentioned by Paul in his letter to the church at Philippi
(4:2). There are several lessons to be learned from their
squabble and the way Paul handled it. Probably he didn't
know which of the two was to blame for the disagreement
so he was careful not to take sides: 'I plead with Euodia
and I plead with Syntyche....' He carefully repeated 'I
plead with' so that it couldn't appear as though he was
expecting one to deal with the situation and not the other.

Secondly, he asks them to 'agree with each other',
literally to be 'like-minded', to have just one mind between
them. But whose mind was it to be? Euodia's or
Syntyche's? In fact neither. They were to have the same
mind as Jesus—to be like-minded in the Lord. Now Paul
had already referred to that idea earlier in his letter. In
chapter 2 he had told *all* the Christians at Philippi that
they ought to have the mind of Christ. The essence of that
mind was humility (read Phil 2:1–11 carefully). So Paul
expressed the general principle first, for everyone to see,
and then he applied it specifically to this one dyad
(remember how one dyad may spoil an entire fellowship?), to Euodia and Syntyche.

We haven't finished with these two ladies yet. How was
this particular disagreement to be sorted out? The answer

to that question comes in Philippians 4:3. They weren't expected to sort it out by themselves. They needed someone else to help them. So Paul writes: 'Yes, and I ask you, loyal yoke-fellow, help these women....'

Actually, that rather stuffy 'loyal yoke-fellow' could well represent a neat pun in Greek. 'Yoke-fellow' in Greek is *synzyge*, and was probably also the name of one of the Christians in the church at Philippi. So Paul is saying: 'Come on now, Synzyge. Live up to your name. Be a "yoke-fellow" to these two ladies. Help them to deal with their burden!' Maybe Synzyge was like so many other Christians: afraid to get involved in settling these squabbles. Paul says: 'Of course you must. It's part of your job.'

Denominations at Corinth

There was a particularly nasty example of squabbling at Corinth. The trouble there was denominations, divisions. Even as early as this in the history of the church people were beginning to choose their human leaders, their big names: Paul, Barnabas, Peter. Not that Paul was consulted about the matter, nor Peter, nor Barnabas.

But Paul wouldn't have it. The point that Paul made in rejecting this particular squabble over personalities was that the church wasn't his, or Peter's. It was God's. One lesson at least we can learn from the disagreement at Corinth is that the Vicar isn't the head of the church, nor the Bishop, nor the Archbishop, nor the Pope, nor the President of Conference, nor anybody else, no matter what sort of title we might create for him. Christ is the head of the church. Not only of the universal church, but also of the local church.

Paul introduces the silly squabble in 1 Corinthians 1:10–13. Further on he asks the question: 'What, after all, is Apollos? And what is Paul?' (3:5). Then he answers his own question. They are servants, people you might expect to find doing some of the tidying up in the synagogue. But the synagogue wouldn't belong to them. They are gardeners (v 6), planting seeds and watering the growing plants. But they wouldn't *own* the garden. They are builders (v 10), mixing mortar, laying bricks. But they wouldn't own the house. They are stewards (4:1), responsible for keeping track of everything in the house. But, again, the house wouldn't be theirs. It was God's house, God's garden, God's church.

And here's the lesson for us all to learn. Even if you are the study leader, it's not *your* house group. It's God's. How we dislike hearing ministers speaking of 'my church'. It isn't. It's God's church and we simply must not encourage people to talk disparagingly of this church, or that church or my church. No good will come of it, but divisions in the house group might easily result. If it *is* a church at all then it's God's church.

Christian cannibalism

Galatians 5:15 speaks of a kind of Christian cannibalism:

> If you keep on biting and devouring each other, watch out or you will be destroyed by each other.

This particular warning draws attention to the danger of allowing disagreements in the house group to go uncorrected. Eventually the cannibals devour one another. The church destroys itself. The following verse provides the alternative to cannibalism:

> So I say, live by the Spirit, and you will not gratify the desires of the sinful nature (Gal 5:16).

If we live by the Spirit we shall be living as Jesus did: for others, and the natural desire of the unsaved human nature, to pull others down, to promote oneself, that natural desire will go.

The weak and the strong

One final example. What should be done when Christians disagree, and it really doesn't seem possible to find any middle way? The answer comes in Romans 14. The section heading in my Bible says 'The Weak and the Strong'.

Oddly enough, you'll find that if you read the chapter carefully the Bible puts things the other way round from the way *we* usually put them. The *strong* Christians do things that other Christians are afraid to do, that other Christians might feel it wrong to do. The weak Christian is the one with all the don'ts.

Romans 14 talks about a problem that wouldn't worry us today. At Corinth there weren't any ordinary butchers' shops. Animals were taken to one of the temples which abounded in the city, dedicated to the god of the temple and then slaughtered. Later the meat was put on sale. Some Christians felt that it was all right to buy the meat, others wouldn't because the meat had been dedicated to a pagan god. The strong Christians pointed out that the pagan gods weren't worth peanuts! Who was right?

Although that particular problem doesn't arise today, and there's not therefore much point in pursuing it, the real issue that gave rise to the problem is still there: the problem of the weak and the strong, the problem posed to a church (or house group) where some Christians feel that they *can* and others feel that they *can't*. Substitute a glass of wine for the plate of beef and you have an argument familiar to many of us. Can you or can't you? Should you or shouldn't you? The list of topics on which Christians tend to disagree fairly strongly is almost endless: cigarettes, going to the theatre, watching TV, pacifism.... Paul's answer is simple: '...let us stop passing judgment on one another' (Rom 14:13).

Actually he has a lot more to say on the subject, but that is an important starting point.

Let's get on with the job of living for God's glory. That

won't be done if we spend time feuding with other Christians. Now that's one thing I've always admired about Billy Graham. Christian people, even Christian leaders, even supposedly evangelical Christian leaders, have been among the first to criticize him. I've listened to interviewers and reporters egging Billy Graham on to hit back. But he never did. I think that's tremendous.

My own feeling is that when I've been used by God as he has been used by God then I'll be qualified to criticize Billy Graham. But of course it's precisely the sort of person who won't criticize Billy Graham who would be used by God!

CHAPTER 10

Preparing for a House-Group Meeting

So you are the study leader for your house group and you have to get down to the task of preparing for next week's session. *Hopefully* you've already had a good session with your monthly training class. *Probably* there's no such thing in your church. So we'll start from scratch. How do you prepare? Where do you begin?

You start with the people who come to the house group. Jesus always suited what he had to say to the people to whom he was speaking. He didn't talk to Nicodemus in the same way as he talked to Martha whose brother had just died. (John 3 and John 11). He didn't talk to the Pharisees in the way that he talked to the ordinary, un-educated people (Luke 11:37–54 and Matthew 5). He talked to the woman he met in Samaria about water, because that was what she was interested in just then. And he talked to the rich ruler about money, because that was what he was always interested in (John 4 and Luke 18:18–25). So we don't plan on talking about things that happen to interest us, but about things that interest others.

In the main, people in house groups don't want a talk about archaeology, ancient history, or Greek society. And that is part of our problem. The Bible is set in another world, the world of Greece and Rome, and Samaria and Babylon and the world of two thousand and more years ago. Somehow we have to move from *that*, from Moses and Abraham, from Peter and Paul, into the twentieth century. It is absolutely vital that you realize that is your task. To bring Bible teaching into Birmingham. The real danger is that because you have to start in Samaria you are very likely to stay in Samaria, answering the questions that people in Samaria asked, but never reaching Birmingham or answering the questions that the people of Birmingham ask.

Let's suppose that you are going to talk about the Communion service and what it means. To make the talk meaningful and understandable, you'll have to talk about how your church actually observes Communion. For Bible study you may have in mind Luke 22:7–23, 1 Corinthians 11:17–34, Exodus 12:1–50 and perhaps other passages too. That's a lot of material.

Now this is where you make an important decision: how much time are you going to give to this subject? I could explain John's gospel in five minutes, five weeks, or five years. I could even spend a lifetime talking about John's gospel without exhausting all that *could* be said about it.

What I could *not* do would be to put all the material for the five years of explanation into my five-minute slot. Which is entirely obvious and only worth saying because so many speakers try to do just that: try to put a quart into a pint pot.

So an important decision has to be made: how much time can I give to this subject? Just one session? Probably. Because there's so much else to be taught in the Church's Education Programme that I can't afford to allocate three months of study to this one subject.

Now then. I have just one evening to talk about the Communion service. But how much time does that actually give me? Let's be practical: if the house group starts at eight o'clock and finishes at nine o'clock I have *not* got one hour for my talk. How much time I *have* got will depend on how I *chunk* the evening. So let's look at this chunking process again.

Although you may never have heard of chunking, if you are a good teacher you will have chunked quite naturally. It's simply a matter of breaking the evening up into digestible bite-sized chunks of time. Just what goes into each chunk is for the study leader to decide. And if he has a prayer leader and a hospitality leader he will certainly want to talk over the evening's chunking with them.

Essentially, the size of the chunks will depend on the people who come to the house group. If they're all students longer might be spent on the study chunk. If the week has been a difficult one for some of them then more time might be given to the prayer chunk. The outline that follows is just one possible pattern:

7.55–8.10	Settling down and prayer.
8.10–8.20	Introduction. This should precede any Bible reading, preparing people for what is going to be read. Most people find this kind of introduction enormously helpful. It fits in with the basic principle of teaching: First I tells 'em what I'm going to tell 'em Then I tells 'em. Then I tells 'em what I told 'em.
8.20–8.25	Reading. The Bible ought to be read in ample chunks, not in single verses. Personally I prefer not to 'read round the group', each person reading one verse. The sense is lost, and some people are embarrassed because they don't read very well.
8.25–8.35	Discuss question 1
8.35–8.45	Discuss question 2
8.45	Prayer time

Of course the times given are only approximate, but they

do give the study leader an indication of how his programme is working out time wise.

Now, with that kind of chunking how much time have
you for your talk about Communion? Ten minutes? For-
tunately it's not quite as desperate as that. If you have
prepared thoroughly you should find that the 'introduction' slot is part of your talk, and that as the Bible is
read it too will do some of your talking for you. (That's
why the introduction ought to tell people what they are
going to hear, so that they will be *listening* for what you
have told them to expect.) The questions also 'talk' as
invariably they need some explanation from the study
leader. Altogether you probably have nearly twenty
minutes of 'talk'. So prepare enough material for twenty
minutes.

Don't despise twenty minutes. Anyone who has been
involved in broadcasting will know how much it's possible
to pack into even a five-minute slot. The secret lies in the
packaging. Leave out all the irrelevant bits and stick to
the subject and you will be surprised at just how much you
can get in.

Let us assume you have decided on the subject of
Communion, and you know the amount of time you have
available, twenty minutes all-in. You also know your
house-group members, and you're going to keep their
faces firmly in mind as you prepare. So what sort of
questions might they have?

Here are just twelve questions I've heard asked about
Communion:

1. Are the bread and wine actually *different* from
   ordinary bread and wine?
2. What happens to what is left over and why?
3. What is meant by taking Communion in an 'unworthy
   manner' (1 Cor 11:27)? And what is this 'judgement'
   that such an action incurs?
4. I've usually heard the minister say something about

'drink you all of this'. Does this mean that it's wicked to leave any wine? (For those churches which use individual Communion cups.)

5. Why is this Communion service so important? People almost seem scared of it. Is it some sort of 'mystery'?

6. Is it wrong for a non-Christian to take Communion? (Sometimes asked by a person who did so many years back and has an uneasy conscience about it. For such a person your answer could be *very* important.)

7. Why don't the Salvation Army have Communion? (*Not* primarily because it involves alcohol, but primarily because the Salvation Army does not see itself as a *church*.)

8. Why do they call Communion 'Eucharist'?

9. Is 'Communion' a sacrament? What *is* a sacrament?

10. How often should I take Communion? Why?

11. Why do some people refuse to eat anything before Communion?

12. If there were, say, a dozen Christians in someone's home could they have a Communion service?

You'll notice that although the answers would be 'theological', the questions actually arise from what people have seen or from what they have heard about other people's practices. Most people work in this way: from practice to theory, not the other way round.

Looking at the questions set out here and thinking about the questions that your folk might ask, would probably suggest which of the many possible passages of the Bible you should concentrate on. Be careful here. If you decide to take 1 Corinthians 11 rather than Luke 22, be sure that you stay fairly firmly in 1 Corinthians 11. Occasional references to other parts of the Bible will be inevitable, but most people find the custom of scooting around all over Old and New Testaments bewildering. They never really get a solid understanding of anything.

Having decided on the appropriate passage of the Bible

to use, study it carefully and prayerfully. Avoid the temptation to turn straight to some learned commentary. You have a greater aid than that: the Holy Spirit. It is his special task to lead us into the truth, but it seems far harder to understand that truth when we've already taken on board the views of some learned professor.

As you read, and as you pray, quickly write down every thought that comes to you. Don't bother about *order* just yet. But don't allow any glimmer of light to escape you. Trap it. Catch it. Nail it down...if you can do that to a glimmer of light! Try, as you read and as you study, to imagine the members of your house group reading it. What might they think? What questions might they ask? And it's at this point that you might need to turn to a commentary if you're honestly not too sure of the answers. But give the Holy Spirit chance to reveal his truth to you *first*.

And finally throw the whole lot...no, not into the fire, but into *order*. Maybe five points that you feel you will want to make. Avoid the trap of attempting to produce five points with fancy rhyming titles, or all beginning with the letter P. That approach often (I'm tempted to say always) leads to mangling the Bible to make it fit the three Ps or whatever you've got.

Still, order is important, so that you will be quite clear about where you are heading, where each part fits in the sequence of teaching.

How much of all this is going to be used? The one certainty ought to be that you won't use it all. A second certainty ought to be that *you* won't say it all. Because a house group meeting is *not* the kind of meeting at which one person speaks, but a small group meeting in which all share. The study leader gives the house group enough hard information to enable the people there to discuss the evening's subject intelligently and work together in finding out the answers to some of the questions. But the study leader doesn't do anything for the group that the group can do for itself.

You see, although people don't actually *know* the answers to their own questions, they probably have almost enough information to enable them to discover the answers. The study leader doesn't write out the questions and then produce all the answers neatly gift-wrapped and tied up in pink ribbon. People don't learn much that way. That is *passive* teaching, teaching that is as easily forgotten as it is easily acquired. So once more we can see how important it is that the study leader is aware of what his house group *does* know, and what they still need to know in order to reach the goal of understanding about the church's Communion service.

What the group does not know has to be supplied:

1. From your introduction *or*
2. From the Bible reading *or*
3. From someone else in the group.

The study leader has the task of seeing that what the group has to learn is given to the group in one of these three ways... or perhaps through some other activity used during the evening. It's something of a jig-saw puzzle. To complete the picture all the pieces will be needed. But it isn't necessary that one person should supply all the pieces.

So now you know what your subject is, you know what the reading will be, you know who your people are and the type of questions they are likely to have, and you know the extra bits of information they must be given before they can really share in the evening's study session. And now you have to work out *where* the additional information is to come from.

The monologue that follows is a kind of conversation with myself, as I think through my task as study leader. Obviously your set of questions and the resources of your group will be different. But this is the kind of monologue that I seem to go through when I prepare a group study:

'I'm pretty sure that none of them will know about the Salvation Army's views on the Communion. *That* isn't in the Bible, so I'll tell them. It's a sort of anecdote, too, so will be fairly light. But it does raise the principle that Communion is really a *church* event and that could lead to a discussion of what we mean by 'church' and whether we might have a Communion service as a house group. (Considers questions 7, 9 and 12 of our list.)

'If we read Matthew 26:27 in a modern translation they'll be able to deal with question 4, about drinking "all of it" themselves although I just might draw attention to it....

'Liz has done some Greek, I know, so I could ask her at some point to explain "Eucharist"...perhaps I should give her a ring first so she's prepared....

'That third question is a good discussion starter because it does set 1 Corinthians 11 in its context at Corinth and will help us to see the problem of rich and poor trying to worship together in one church. This wretched class business...working class, middle class, upper class...this could help to draw out the significance of calling it "Communion"...with God and with one another. The idea that we are a family and our relationships with one another do affect our relationship with our Father....'

And so your preparation proceeds. Thought, prayer, a quick note. It all takes *far* more time than preparing a sermon—it's a much more difficult exercise. But if the preparation is well done then there will be *real* learning.

Asking questions

Discussion is a vital part of G2 house groups. Discussion arises out of good, relevant, provocative, productive teaching and out of the careful use of questions. Always prepare some questions so that if the group doesn't produce its own you will have some to get discussion going. Produce more questions than you are likely to need so that you have freedom to choose the questions from your list that are relevant and discard those which turn out in fact to be unnecessary.

There are three basic types of question:

1. Factual questions

These are probably the most used, and are certainly the easiest to produce, but they are the least useful of the three types. If you are studying John 2 it's easy to ask where the wedding took place, but you can't do anything much with the answer when you've got it.

2. Opinion questions

You can see how effective this type of question is from Matthew 21:25. Jesus asked: 'John's baptism, where did it come from?'

Of course, if you are going to use opinion questions, be quite sure that your house group *has* an opinion on the subject, or at least that they could easily form an opinion. So you may need to give some information before asking opinion questions such as: 'Do you think that Paul was right in arguing with Peter in public like that?' (see Gal 2:11–21), and, 'Do you think that Matthew 5:42 means that the Christian should always give to people who ask for help and always lend money to anyone who wants to borrow it?'

When asking opinion questions it is usually best to try to set the question in the context of an actual event. So you might put the last question differently: 'You are a Christian and a beggar comes knocking at your door. What would you do if he asked you for your coat?' Or, 'You are a Christian and your neighbour comes round trying to borrow two hundred pounds from you and you have that much in the bank. Would you lend it to him?'

3. Illustration questions

An illustration doesn't ask for facts about the problem

being discussed, nor for an opinion about the problem, but for an experience that illustrates the problem. So if you are talking about this question of giving to beggars you might invite the minister to come and talk about his experiences with beggars.

So there are different types of question, and it's a good thing to use some of each type during the evening's discussion. Finally, three important principles to be remembered when constructing questions. Firstly, questions must be pitched at the right level—the level suited to your house group. If they're too difficult the group may be unable to answer them, but if they are too easy they may not try to answer them because they'll suspect a trick.

And that leads to the second principle: the questions must be honest questions, not trick questions. The Nicene Creed didn't really come from Nicea, and the Athanasian Creed was almost certainly not written by Athanasius, but making adults look foolish by asking trick questions is one sure way of guaranteeing that no one answers *any* question.

Thirdly, avoid 'omnibus questions'. Omnibus questions are questions that pick up fresh passengers at every pause, for example, 'Do you think that Jesus was simply trying to embarrass the priests by that question mentioned in...is it Matthew 21...or was he actually trying to teach them something and *that's* why he puts it the way he does, in just two sentences? Or maybe the two sentences are just a problem of translation, do you think, Liz? But in any case don't you think that brief questions like that carry much more punch than long questions...or don't you agree?'

Using notes

You'll have to make up your own mind about using notes. Some people make their notes on small cards, some prefer a notebook (if so, use a lie-flat spiral-bound notebook), some use just headings, others prefer to have fairly full notes. In all this there is just one essential: you must be able to use them! It's very embarrassing to everyone in the house group when the study leader's raft of notes keep fluttering to the floor reducing the original order to total chaos.

For myself I use a clip-board. It has a clip fastener on the right hand side, and a plastic pocket on the left. I keep my notes for the study session on the right hand side, and if I do have more than one page of notes I have each sheet *boldly* numbered.

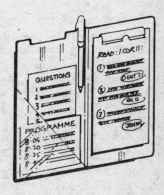

On the left hand side of the clip-board I have one sheet with the evening's chunking noted on it including a clear indication of when each chunk should begin. A second sheet has my collection of questions. I also have a pen clipped in somewhere. It's a simple system, easy to use—even when you are sitting in an armchair.

CHECK SHEET NUMBER THREE

These questions all relate to chapters 7–10 of this book.

1. Write down the names of three neighbours, relatives or friends who live near you but are not committed Christians.
   Have you asked them to come to your church or house group?

   Yes _____
   No _____

   If not, what would make it possible for you to do so? _____

   _____

   _____

2. Which of the following passages would you choose for a study of people prejudice?

   a) Acts 10 _____
   b) James 2:1–13 _____
   c) Luke 17:11–19 _____
   d) Galatians 2:11–16 _____
   e) Ephesians 2:11–22 _____

   (There's no 'right' answer to this question, but each passage might fit a different situation. It's worth discussing this particular question with a group. Such a discussion would show you how much you have learned practically from reading this book.)

3. What is meant by 'chunking'? _____

   _____

4. Ask half a dozen of your Christian friends to write down two questions each about Communion.
   Now compare *their* questions with my list in chapter ten.

   a) Which of my questions have they left out?
   b) What new questions have you got?
   c) Can you explain the differences?
   d) Can you answer their questions?

Something More to Read

In this book I've been discussing house groups which ought to form part of the normal life of the local church. So you may well want to know more about the activity of the local church. Similarly, house groups are just part of our total system of communication, and you may well want to learn more about human communication. And thirdly all of this book assumes that the reader is a Christian. But you might want to know more about what Christianity is.

I'm drawing your attention to three of my own books covering these three subjects, partly because I know that they are all written in much the same style and at much the same level as this one. So if you've persevered with this book then you may find the others helpful:

> *Church Alive!* (Inter-Varsity Press)
> *Look Who's Talking* (Kingsway Publications)
> *This Is Christianity* (Inter-Varsity Press)

The Bible Society has published a most useful series called *Using the Bible Series*. Number nine in the series is called *In groups*, by Roberta Hestenes. It is full of helpful ideas, especially expanding on chapter six of this book.

Pioneer International Publishing have a useful series of booklets on individual books of the Bible, called *Dis-*

covering Bible Books. Each study includes practical questions which should help to get a study group going.

Another book on house groups, *Wednesday Night at Eight,* is by Richard and Susan Haydon-Knowell, published by Kingsway Publications.